Vocabulary Power

MW01109511

Teacher's Guide
GRADE 2

Printed in the United States of America

ISBN 0-15-320246-7

5 6 7 8 9 10 082 2003 2002

Table of Contents

Introduction

Research Findings

Research documents the relationship between vocabulary knowledge, reading comprehension, and oral and written expression. The more words children acquire, the better chance they will have for success in reading, writing, and spelling. *Vocabulary Power* is a **vocabulary development program** that will promote children's "word consciousness"—their awareness of and interest in words.

From research we know that children learn between 1,000 and 5,000 words per year— and the average child learns about 3,000 words. We also know that wide reading is the most effective technique for increasing vocabulary. However, practice has demonstrated that 300–500 words per year can be taught through direct instruction.

A vocabulary program must help children experience words by

- **hearing** and **seeing** words used;
- **discussing** and **defining** meanings of words;
- **reading** and **writing** words in meaningful contexts.

In addition to helping children broaden and expand their vocabularies, a vocabulary program must also help them learn techniques for independent vocabulary acquisition.

lullaby

serenade

jingle

Fostering Vocabulary Development

In *Vocabulary Power* children learn through daily activities that actively involve them in listening, speaking, reading, and writing. These activities

- **present** them with words from their own oral vocabularies, words that they also need to decode and to read;
- **introduce** them to new concepts and words, and to new labels for familiar concepts;
- **show** them how words are properly used and how our language works;
- **provide** opportunities for discussions, an important dimension of vocabulary development.

The activities in *Vocabulary Power* encourage comprehension and associative thinking. Children learn both the definitions of the vocabulary words and how the words function in different contexts. Their tasks may include

- ☑ to identify or supply synonyms, antonyms, or related words;
- ☑ to generate lists of new or known words;
- ☑ to classify, categorize, compare, contrast, illustrate;
- ☑ to create original sentences.

Many tasks are open-ended to encourage discussion and sharing of ideas.

How to Use This Book

Overview

The **instructional plan** for the *Vocabulary Power Teacher's Guide* introduces five vocabulary words per week for 36 weeks. You can find the lists of these vocabulary words in the Weekly Instructional Plans section of this guide on pages T6–T11. Some words in these lists appear in boldface type. These are designated as Power Words because they provide the springboard for learning the rest of the Words of the Week and for relating the Words of the Week to each other.

The *Vocabulary Power Teacher's Guide* also includes

- ideas for informal assessment;
- activities and word lists to engage learners;
- 180 reproducible Word Cards to be reproduced and cut apart for use in whole class or in small group instruction.

See pages T12–T24 for additional ideas and suggestions.

Weekly Plan

Each weekly plan provides five days of vocabulary assignments. As you work through these assignments, you can contribute to children's success by

- using the words throughout the day as part of your own vocabulary;
- having children look for the words in newspapers and magazines;
- using the words in classroom contests or as part of classroom business;
- maintaining a chart of "Word Sightings" in the classroom;
- keeping dictionaries on hand and encouraging children to use them;
- encouraging children to keep their own word lists and to use words from these lists in their daily writing.

The Weekly Instructional Plans on pages T6–T11 of this guide contain specific plans based upon the following model:

DAY ❶	Introduce and discuss the Power Word.
DAY ❷	Introduce the remaining four Words of the Week. Complete the first worksheet.
DAY ❸	Review words. Complete the second worksheet.
DAY ❹	Review words. Complete the third worksheet.
DAY ❺	Review words. Do an assessment activity.

Informal Assessment Ideas

WEEKLY
Have children demonstrate knowledge using one or more of the following techniques.

Kid Watching
Observe children daily in informal situations.

- Do you hear them use the words in playground talk, in conversations, or in classroom discussions?
- Do they attempt to use the words in their own writing?
- Do they mention seeing or hearing the words on television or radio, or seeing the words in printed materials?

Self-Assessment/Peer Assessment
As words are introduced each week, have children create a Rating Chart with the following headings: *Know this word / Have seen or heard this word / Don't know this word.* Have them return to this chart periodically to make adjustments or to update their responses. Suggest that children determine if they need to spend more time with any of the words.

Have children maintain a log of *when, where,* or *how* they saw or heard any of the Words of the Week, or maintain a chart in the classroom where you can record "Word Sightings."

Assessment Activities
Plan activities to have children demonstrate their knowledge and understanding of the Words of the Week. The activities may or may not be timed. You might have students match each word with its definition or have them define a word in one of these ways:

- ☑ use the word in a sentence
- ☑ write another word that has a similar meaning
- ☑ write a word that has a meaning opposite to the word
- ☑ indicate its semantic features (prefix, suffix, compound word, and so on)
- ☑ provide an example (written or drawn)
- ☑ provide a statement of how the example compares/contrasts to another word
- ☑ show the relationship of a part to the whole or vice versa
- ☑ present the word in a graphic manner that shows its meaning

END OF UNIT
Have children demonstrate knowledge through one of the following techniques:

Conduct an Open Sort
Select a representative group of words and have children organize the words into categories of their own choosing.

Conduct a Closed Sort
Distribute to children a representative group of words and a list of categories. Have them categorize the words appropriately.

Weekly Instructional Plans

Chapter 1	**WORDS OF THE WEEK:** capture, clutch, grab, grasp, **seize**
DAY 1	WORD MEANING Introduce and define *seize* (to take, to grab onto). Have volunteers demonstrate the meaning by seizing various classroom items.
DAY 2 *p. 1*	SYNONYMS Write: *seize, bring, grab.* **Which of the words have the same meaning?**
DAY 3 *p. 2*	WORD ENDINGS List: *seize, seizes, seized.* **What other endings can be added to *seize*?**
DAY 4 *p. 3*	FIGURATIVE LANGUAGE Write: *I was seized by a need for ice cream.* **What does this sentence mean?**
DAY 5	GRAPHICS/ART Invite children to make posters to illustrate the saying "Seize the Day!"

Chapter 4	**WORDS OF THE WEEK:** entirely, mostly, partly, totally, **wholly**
DAY 1	WORD MEANING Introduce and define *wholly* (totally, completely). Ask children if the sky is wholly, or totally, blue.
DAY 2 *p. 10*	RELATED WORDS Write: *wholly, happy, totally.* **Which two words have the same meaning?**
DAY 3 *p. 11*	WORD FAMILIES Write *wholly.* **What is the base word? What ending has been added to *whole* to make *wholly*?**
DAY 4 *p. 12*	HOMOPHONES Write: *This book is wholly new.* Swiss cheese is *holey.* Discuss how the underlined words are alike and different.
DAY 5	RHYMING WORDS Write: *Humpty-Dumpty was wholly roly-poly.* **Which words rhyme?** Interested children can illustrate the sentence. Others can make a list of rhyming words.

Chapter 2	**WORDS OF THE WEEK:** anthem, folk song, jingle, **lullaby**, serenade
DAY 1	WORD MEANING Introduce and define *lullaby* (a kind of song). Ask: **When does a mother sing a lullaby?** Invite volunteers to sing a lullaby such as "Rock-a-Bye-Baby."
DAY 2 *p. 4*	CONTEXT CLUES Write: *The lullaby made me feel sleepy.* **What words help you understand *lullaby*?**
DAY 3 *p. 5*	CLASSIFY AND CATEGORIZE Write *song* and *dance.* **Which word tells what a lullaby is?**
DAY 4 *p. 6*	COMPARE/CONTRAST Write *lullaby* and *anthem.* **How are they alike? Different?**
DAY 5	PERFORM Invite groups of volunteers to sing a favorite song. Discuss the various kinds of songs performed.

Chapter 5	**WORDS OF THE WEEK:** agreement, disagreement, disharmony, **harmony**, togetherness
DAY 1	WORD MEANING Write: *When we work together we are in harmony.* Discuss specific times when children have worked in harmony.
DAY 2 *p. 13*	SYNONYMS/ANTONYMS Write: *harmony, together, apart.* **Which two words have similar meanings? Which are opposites?**
DAY 3 *p. 14*	PREFIXES/SUFFIXES Write: *harmony, disharmony.* **How does adding *dis-* to the beginning of harmony change the meaning?**
DAY 4 *p. 15*	RELATED WORDS Write: *The four singers sang in harmony.* **What does harmony have to do with singing and music?**
DAY 5	COMPARISON **Would you rather sing in harmony or work in harmony with classmates? Why?**

Chapter 3	**WORDS OF THE WEEK:** burrow, cave, lair, lodge, roost
DAY 1	WORD MEANING Introduce and define *burrow* (home dug in the ground by an animal). **Name some animals that dig burrows** (rabbit, mole).
DAY 2 *p. 7*	CONTEXT CLUES Write: *The mole is safe and snug in its burrow.* **What words help you understand burrow?**
DAY 3 *p. 8*	MULTI-MEANING WORDS Write: *Do you burrow under the covers on cold nights?* **What does burrow mean?**
DAY 4 *p. 9*	CONTENT-AREA WORDS Write: *Science, Math, Gym.* **In which class would you learn about burrows?**
DAY 5	GRAPHICS/ART Have children make a book about animal homes, illustrating and labeling the animal homes, such as a burrow.

Chapter 6	**WORDS OF THE WEEK:** brightest, **glossiest**, shiniest, sleekest, smoothest
DAY 1	WORD MEANING Introduce and define the word *glossiest* (most shiny). Write *The red dancing shoes were the glossiest of all.* **How would you draw these dancing shoes?**
DAY 2 *p. 16*	WORD FAMILIES List: *glossy, glossier, glossiest.* **What is the base word? What endings were added to the base word?**
DAY 3 *p. 17*	COMPARE/CONTRAST Discuss: **What animal has the glossiest fur? Why do you think that?**
DAY 4 *p. 18*	EXPAND WORD MEANING Write: *Mom painted the walls with gloss paint.* **Why would she do that? What is gloss paint?**
DAY 5	ANTONYMS **Make a list of words that mean the opposite of *glossy, bright, shiny, sleek, smooth.***

Chapter 7	WORDS OF THE WEEK: **countryside**, farmland, field, meadow, pasture
DAY 1	WORD MEANING Write: *countryside*. **What might you see in the countryside?**
DAY 2 *p. 19*	CONTENT-AREA WORDS Write: *Farms, Cities, Numbers*. **Which topic would include the countryside? Why?**
DAY 3 *p. 20*	COMPOUND WORDS Write: *countryside*. **What two words make up this compound word?**
DAY 4 *p. 21*	ANALOGIES Write: *field-country, sidewalk-_____*. **You can see a field in the country. Where can you see a sidewalk?**
DAY 5	GRAPHICS/ART **Draw a mural of a countryside. Attach labels to various features in your mural.**

Chapter 10	WORDS OF THE WEEK: **ambassador**, chairperson, mayor, officer, president
DAY 1	WORD MEANING Introduce and define *ambassador* (a messenger). Ask volunteers to act as ambassadors to other classrooms. Have them deliver messages.
DAY 2 *p. 28*	TITLES FOR PEOPLE Write: *Jane Starr is an ambassador to another country. I think Ambassador Starr works hard.* **What do these sentences tell you about the meaning of ambassador?**
DAY 3 *p. 29*	ABBREVIATIONS List: *Ambassador Starr, Amb. Starr*. **What are the first three letters in Ambassador? What does Amb. mean?**
DAY 4 *p. 30*	EXPAND WORD MEANING Write: *Bob is an ambassador for kindness.* **What does this sentence mean?**
DAY 5	PERFORM Provide opportunities for children to act as group leaders. Encourage them to give themselves titles such as "Mayor of Math City."

Chapter 8	WORDS OF THE WEEK: adult, **cocoons**, cycle, larvae, pupa
DAY 1	WORD MEANING Write: *cocoons*. **Cocoons are wrappings that keep baby silkworms safe. What other creatures use a cocoon?**
DAY 2 *p. 22*	CONTENT-AREA WORDS Write: *Math, Science, Music*. **In which class might you learn about cocoons?**
DAY 3 *p. 23*	RELATED WORDS Write: *cocoon, shelter*. **Why do these words go together? Name some other shelters.**
DAY 4 *p. 24*	WORD FAMILIES List: *cocoon, cocoons; larva, larvae*. **Which words mean one? Which words mean more than one?**
DAY 5	EXEMPLIFICATION Have children draw pictures of the stages in the life of a butterfly and label the stages.

Chapter 11	WORDS OF THE WEEK: cattail, cowhand, pigtail, **rattlesnake**, turtleneck
DAY 1	WORD MEANING Write: *rattlesnake*. **How do you think this snake got its name?**
DAY 2 *p. 31*	COMPOUND WORDS Write: *rattlesnake*. **What two words are combined to form this word?**
DAY 3 *p. 32*	WORD FAMILIES List: *rattlesnake, snakeskin, blacksnake*. **Why do we say that these words are in the same word family?**
DAY 4 *p. 33*	ONOMATOPOEIA Write: *moo, meow, oink*. **Which word tells the sound a cat makes? A pig? A cow?**
DAY 5	COMPOUND WORDS List: *cat, tail, house, fly, stick, jump, cow, snow, rain*. **Make a list of compound words. Here are some words you might use.**

Chapter 9	WORDS OF THE WEEK: bronco, lasso, **rodeo**, saddle, steer
DAY 1	WORD MEANING Write: *rodeo*. Talk about what a rodeo is. **What might you see at a rodeo?**
DAY 2 *p. 25*	CONTEXT CLUES Write: *My dad won the bull-riding contest at the rodeo*. **What clues help you understand what a rodeo is?**
DAY 3 *p. 26*	WORD ORIGINS Write: *rodeo*. **The word rodeo is a Spanish word that comes from Mexico. What other Spanish words do you know?**
DAY 4 *p. 27*	CLASSIFY/CATEGORIZE Write *Toys, Sports, Cities*. **In which category does rodeo belong? Why?**
DAY 5	MULTIPLE-MEANING WORDS Have children illustrate the following phrases: a steer, to steer; a saddle, to saddle; a lasso, to lasso.

Chapter 12	WORDS OF THE WEEK: delve, **explored**, inquire, observe, quest
DAY 1	WORD MEANING Write: *Rosie explored the backyard at her new house*. **What do you do when you explore?** (look, search)
DAY 2 *p. 34*	RELATED WORDS Write *explored, searched, treasure*. **These words go together. Which two words have the same meaning? Why does the word treasure belong in this group?**
DAY 3 *p. 35*	WORD FAMILIES List: *explore, explored, explorer*. **Which word is the base word? What is another word in this word family?**
DAY 4 *p. 36*	EXPAND WORD MEANING Write: *Astronauts explore space. You can explore space at the library.* **How are these kinds of exploring alike? How are they different?**
DAY 5	COMPARISON **Would you rather explore or observe a cave? Why?**

Chapter 13	WORDS OF THE WEEK: flicker, **flutter**, quiver, shiver, sputter

DAY 1   WORD MEANING   Write: *flutter.* **How does a butterfly flutter?** Have volunteers act out the meaning of *flutter.*

DAY 2   *p. 37*   RELATED WORDS   Write: *flow, flutter, flap.* **Which two words describe the same kind of movement?**

DAY 3   *p. 38*   MULTI-MEANING WORDS   Write: *I'm in a flutter when I'm late for school.* **What does being in a flutter mean in this sentence?**

DAY 4   *p. 39*   RHYMING WORDS   Write: *flutter, sputter.* **How are these words alike? Name another word that rhymes.**

DAY 5   ALLITERATION   Write: *Butterflies flit, flap, flitter, and flutter in a flurry.* Discuss which words have similar meanings. Invite children to say the tongue twister faster and faster. **Make a list of words that begin like *sputter*. Write your own tongue twister.**

Chapter 16	WORDS OF THE WEEK: circular, orbit, **revolving**, spinning, spiral

DAY 1   WORD MEANING   Introduce and define *revolving.* Have children act out the meaning by moving in a circle around their chairs.

DAY 2   *p. 46*   CONTEXT CLUES   Write: *The planets are <u>revolving</u> around the sun.* **What word or words help you understand the meaning of revolving?**

DAY 3   *p. 47*   WORD FAMILIES   List: *revolve, revolving.* **What is the base word? What other endings can you add to revolve?**

DAY 4   *p. 48*   MULTI-MEANING WORDS   Write: *My interests revolve around sports.* **What does this sentence mean?**

DAY 5   SYNONYMS   Have children make a word web for *revolve* by writing words with similar meanings.

Chapter 14	WORDS OF THE WEEK: communicate, confer, **consulting**, converse, recommend

DAY 1   WORD MEANING   Write *consulting,* and talk about its meaning. (asking, exchanging ideas with) **With whom might you consult?**

DAY 2   *p. 40*   SYNONYMS   Write: *consulting, asking, forgetting.* **Which two words have similar meanings?**

DAY 3   *p. 41*   WORD FAMILIES   List: *consulted, consulting.* **How are these words alike? Different?**

DAY 4   *p. 42*   ABBREVIATIONS   Write: *Let's <u>consult</u> Dr. Appleton.* **What does the underlined word mean? Why would you consult a doctor?**

DAY 5   CLASSIFY/CATEGORIZE   List children's interests, such as animals or stars. **Whom would you consult to learn more about your interest?** Use the following during discussion: *communicate, confer, converse, recommend.*

Chapter 17	WORDS OF THE WEEK: anchored, attached, connected, **fastened**, united

DAY 1   WORD MEANING   Introduce and define *fastened* (joined, connected). **Why is it important to have your seatbelt fastened?**

DAY 2   *p. 49*   SYNONYMS   Write: *fastened.* **Name words that have a similar meaning.**

DAY 3   *p. 50*   PREFIXES   List: *fastened, <u>un</u>fastened, <u>re</u>fastened.* Have children use paper clips and papers to show word meaning.

DAY 4   *p. 51*   EXPAND WORD MEANING   Listen: *Josie fastened her eyes on the TV.* **What does this sentence mean? Describe or tell what Josie did.**

DAY 5   RELATED WORDS   **Make a list of items that could be used as fasteners** (paper clips, buttons, snaps, zipper, and so on).

Chapter 15	WORDS OF THE WEEK: category, family, similar, **species**, specimen

DAY 1   WORD MEANING   Introduce and define *species* (group, category). **Name some species, or kinds, of dogs.**

DAY 2   *p. 43*   CONTENT-AREA WORDS   Write: *There are many <u>species</u> of animals and plants.* **In which class would you learn about species: Math, Art, or Science?**

DAY 3   *p. 44*   MULTI-MEANING WORDS   Write: *A tiger is a species of the cat <u>family</u>. I am the oldest child in my <u>family</u>.* Discuss the different meanings of *family.*

DAY 4   *p. 45*   ANALOGIES   List: *tiger-cat, rose-_____.* **A tiger is a kind of cat. A rose is a kind of . . .** (flower).

DAY 5   CLASSIFY/CATEGORIZE   Write: *Animal, Plant, Family Member, Toy.* **Write or draw three or more things that belong in each category.**

Chapter 18	WORDS OF THE WEEK: beasts, beings, **creatures**, critters, varmints

DAY 1   WORD MEANING   Write: *Bears are furry <u>creatures</u>.* Discuss the meaning of *creatures.* (living beings, animals)

DAY 2   *p. 52*   RELATED WORDS   Write: *creatures, spoons, animals.* **Which two words go together? Why?**

DAY 3   *p. 53*   EXPAND WORD MEANING   Write: *A warm, snug bed is a <u>creature</u> comfort.* Discuss the meaning of *creature comfort.*

DAY 4   *p. 54*   REGIONALISMS   Write: *creature, critter.* **The word critter is a form of the word creature. In some places, people call horses and cows critters. Why do you think people started saying critter for creature?** (similar sounds)

DAY 5   WORD USAGE   Small groups can make up a story about a make-believe creature. Encourage them to include the words *beast, being, critter, varmint.*

Chapter 19	**WORDS OF THE WEEK: considerate**, courteous, mannerly, polite, thoughtful
DAY 1	WORD MEANING Introduce and define *considerate*. **What are some examples of considerate things that people do for each other?**
DAY 2 p. 55	ANTONYMS Write *considerate* and *thoughtless* on the board. Explain that these two words have opposite meanings. **What other antonym pairs can you name?**
DAY 3 p. 56	CONTEXT CLUES Say: **The considerate student helped her friend.** Have partners act out situations that show considerate behavior.
DAY 4 p. 57	WORD FAMILIES Write *consider/considerate* on the board. **What ending was added to consider?** Have a volunteer underline it. Explain that *consider* means "to think about." The *-ate* changes the meaning to "acting a way that thinks [about others]."
DAY 5	RELATED WORDS Have children make a word map for *considerate*. They should add adjectives that describe a considerate person.

Chapter 20	**WORDS OF THE WEEK:** appetizing, delicious, flavorful, **luscious**, savory
DAY 1	WORD MEANING Introduce and define *luscious* (delicious, tasty). Discuss luscious foods.
DAY 2 p. 58	SYNONYMS Write *luscious* on the board. Help children name words with similar meanings.
DAY 3 p. 59	RELATED WORDS Discuss what makes food luscious, such as sweetness.
DAY 4 p. 60	EXPAND WORD MEANING Remind children that *luscious* describes foods. Discuss what other things *luscious* might describe.
DAY 5	CONTENT-AREA WORDS Ask children to write a menu that contains their favorite foods. Suggest that they use words such as *luscious* to describe the dishes.

Chapter 21	**WORDS OF THE WEEK:** coil, swirl, twirl, twist, **whirl**
DAY 1	WORD MEANING Introduce *whirl* (spin). Have children act out the meaning by whirling their fingers in the air.
DAY 2 p. 61	SYNONYMS Write: *whirl, climb, spin*. **Which two words have similar meanings?**
DAY 3 p. 62	RHYMING WORDS List: *whirl, girl, swirl*. **How are these words alike? What is another word that rhymes?**
DAY 4 p. 63	BLENDED WORDS Write: *twist+whirl=twirl*. **What parts of twist and whirl are blended to make the word twirl?**
DAY 5	FIGURATIVE LANGUAGE Have children draw and label pictures to show when they have been "in a dizzy whirl."

Chapter 22	**WORDS OF THE WEEK:** countless, endless, **infinite**, unlimited, vast
DAY 1	WORD MEANING Introduce and define *infinite* (too big to measure or count). Read this sentence: **A cow has an infinite number of legs. Why is it untrue?**
DAY 2 p. 64	SYNONYMS Write: *There are almost endless numbers of stars.* **What word has the same meaning as infinite?**
DAY 3 p. 65	WORD FAMILIES Write: *infinite, infinity, infant*. **Which words belong to the same word family? Why?**
DAY 4 p. 66	FIGURATIVE LANGUAGE Write: *It will take an infinity to finish this work!* **What does this sentence mean?**
DAY 5	SUFFIXES Write: *endless*. Have children brainstorm a list of other words that end with *-less*. Encourage children to draw pictures to illustrate some of their words.

Chapter 23	**WORDS OF THE WEEK:** hasty, **quicker**, rapid, speedily, swiftest
DAY 1	WORD MEANING Write: *quicker*. **Which is quicker, a snail or a mouse? What is even quicker?**
DAY 2 p. 67	RELATED WORDS Write: *quicker — size? speed? shape?* **What does the word quicker tell about: something's size, speed, or shape?**
DAY 3 p. 68	WORD FAMILIES Write: *quicker, quacking, quickest*. **Which two words belong in the same word family? Why?**
DAY 4 p. 69	SYNONYMS Write: *hasty, rapid, slow*. **Which two words have a similar meaning?**
DAY 5	ABBREVIATIONS **Writing the abbreviation is often quicker than writing the complete word. Make a list of all the abbreviations you know. Hint: think about titles of people, days of the week, and months of the year.**

Chapter 24	**WORDS OF THE WEEK: dignified**, formal, noble, regal, royal
DAY 1	WORD MEANING Write: *dignified*. **What does dignified mean?** (grand, important) **Do you think penguins look dignified? Why or why not?**
DAY 2 p. 70	CONTEXT CLUES Write: *The speakers stood tall and spoke well. They seemed quite <u>dignified</u>.* **What clues help you understand the meaning of dignified?**
DAY 3 p. 71	CLASSIFY/CATEGORIZE Write: *dignified, undignified*. Have children categorize these behaviors: standing tall and straight, slouching. **What other words have the same base word as dignified?**
DAY 4 p. 72	TITLES FOR PEOPLE Say: **The president and the queen look dignified. Which words name people? Name some other titles for people.**
DAY 5	CLASSIFY/CATEGORIZE Have children introduce themselves or make an announcement in a formal manner. Remind them to look and act dignified.

Chapter 25	WORDS OF THE WEEK: action, connection, **contribution**, prediction, transportation
DAY 1	WORD MEANING Introduce and define *contribution* (something given). **How can you make a contribution when we talk about a book?**
DAY 2 p. 73	WORD FAMILIES Write: *contribute, contribution*. **Are these two words in the same word family? How do you know?**
DAY 3 p. 74	SUFFIXES Write: *act, acted, action*. **What is the base word? What endings have been added to the base word?**
DAY 4 p. 75	ANALOGIES Write: *A contribution is something you give. An action is something you _____.* (do) **What word completes this sentence?**
DAY 5	GRAPHICS/ART Invite children to make a book about different kinds of transportation. Have each child label his or her contribution.

Chapter 28	WORDS OF THE WEEK: advise, direct, **guided**, led, taught
DAY 1	WORD MEANING Write: *guided*. Talk about its meaning. **What does *guided* mean? When might you guide a pencil?**
DAY 2 p. 82	RELATED WORDS List: *guided, taught, school*. **These words go together. Which two words have similar meanings? Why does the word *school* belong in this group?**
DAY 3 p. 83	EXPAND WORD MEANING Write: *My mom is a museum guide*. **What does *guide* mean in this sentence?**
DAY 4 p. 84	HOMOPHONES Write: *led, lead*. **Led means "guided." Lead is a metal. How are the two words the same? How are the words different?**
DAY 5	COMPARISON **If you were learning to ride a two-wheel bike, would you want someone to guide you or direct you? Why?**

Chapter 26	WORDS OF THE WEEK: frayed, **ragged**, shaggy, tattered, uneven
DAY 1	WORD MEANING Write: *ragged*. Talk about its meaning. **How do you think a ragged blanket looks?**
DAY 2 p. 76	SYNONYMS Write: *ragged, neat, shaggy*. **Which two words have similar meanings?**
DAY 3 p. 77	FIGURATIVE LANGUAGE Write: *I look like a Raggedy-Andy*. **What does this sentence mean? When might someone say such a sentence?**
DAY 4 p. 78	RHYMING WORDS Write: *ragged, jagged*. **How are these words alike? Name another word that rhymes.**
DAY 5	ALLITERATION Write: *I ran down a ragged-rugged-rough-rocky road*. **Make a list of words that begin like *frayed*. Write a sentence using your words to describe a friend, fruit, or french fry.**

Chapter 29	WORDS OF THE WEEK: **angrily**, gracefully, hungrily, noisily, playfully
DAY 1	WORD MEANING Write: *angrily*. **What does the word *angrily* mean?** Have volunteers ask the question angrily.
DAY 2 p. 85	CONTEXT CLUES Write: *The boy shouted and angrily slammed the door*. **What clues help you understand the meaning of *angrily*?**
DAY 3 p. 86	SUFFIXES List: *angry, angrily*. **How does adding the ending -ly change the meaning of angry?**
DAY 4 p. 87	ANTONYMS Write: *angrily, sweetly*. **Do these two words have the same or opposite meanings?** Ask volunteers to say "I know" angrily and then sweetly.
DAY 5	ONOMATOPOEIA Have children make a growling sound such as g-r-r-r. Ask volunteers to growl angrily . . . hungrily . . . noisily . . . playfully.

Chapter 27	WORDS OF THE WEEK: demonstrate, display, illustrate, model, present
DAY 1	WORD MEANING Write: *demonstrate*. **What does *demonstrate* mean?** (show how to do something) **What could a firefighter demonstrate?**
DAY 2 p. 79	RELATED WORDS Write: *demonstrate, explain, teachers*. **These words go together. Which words have similar meanings? Why does the word *teachers* belong in this group?**
DAY 3 p. 80	MULTI-MEANING WORDS Write: *I can illustrate how to swim. I can illustrate a story.* Discuss the two meanings of *illustrate*.
DAY 4 p. 81	HOMOGRAPHS Write: *I'd like to present you a present*. **How are the underlined words alike? How are they different?**
DAY 5	PERFORM Invite volunteers to demonstrate how to do or make something.

Chapter 30	WORDS OF THE WEEK: interact, intercom, interleaf, **international**, Internet
DAY 1	WORD MEANING Introduce and define *international*. (relating to different nations, countries, cultures) Ask children to name countries they know about.
DAY 2 p. 88	CONTEXT CLUES Write: *Everyone in the world likes to dance. Dancing is international.* **What clues help you understand the meaning of *international*?**
DAY 3 p. 89	PREFIXES Write: *Each country has one national anthem, but singing is international.* Help children understand that *national* refers to one country, and *international* refers to many different countries.
DAY 4 p. 90	CLIPPED WORDS Write: *intercommunication*. **How is the word *intercom* like an abbreviation?**
DAY 5	JARGON Write: *The Internet is international*. With children, brainstorm a list of words that relate to communicating by computer.

Chapter 31	WORDS OF THE WEEK: anteater, groundhog, **mockingbird**, starfish, stingray
DAY 1	WORD MEANING Write: *mock, mocking, mockingbird.* **One meaning of *mock* is "to copy." How do you think the mockingbird got its name?** (A mockingbird can mimic, or copy, the calls of other birds.)
DAY 2 p. 91	COMPOUND WORDS Write: *mocking + bird = mockingbird.* **Mockingbirds mock the sounds of other birds. Do you think *mockingbird* is a good name for this bird?**
DAY 3 p. 92	CLASSIFY/CATEGORIZE List: *crow, mockingbird, robin.* **What kind of animal do these words name? What other animals fly?**
DAY 4 p. 93	REGIONALISMS Write: *Groundhogs are also called woodchucks.* **Why do you think the same animal has a different name in a different part of the country?**
DAY 5	COMPOUND WORDS Have children dictate a list of animal names. **Use these words to make your own list of compound words.**

Chapter 34	WORDS OF THE WEEK: fabulous, fantastic, **marvelous**, splendid, superb
DAY 1	WORD MEANING Write: *Bobby had a marvelous time _____.* Discuss the meaning of *marvelous.* (great, wonderful) **Have children dictate phrases to complete the sentence.**
DAY 2 p. 100	SYNONYMS Write: *marvelous, awful, super.* **Which two words have similar meanings? Which word has a meaning opposite to the other two?**
DAY 3 p. 101	WORD ORIGINS List: *marvelous, wonder, terror.* **The word *marvelous* comes from a very old word. What do you think that old word means: *wonder* or *terror*? Why?**
DAY 4 p. 102	ANALOGIES Write: *Marvelous* is the opposite of *terrible. Happy* is the opposite of _____. **What word completes the sentence?** (sad)
DAY 5	CLASSIFY/CATEGORIZE Have children draw and write about the books they have read. Have them categorize the books as "marvelous" or "so-so."

Chapter 32	WORDS OF THE WEEK: bellow, **croak**, hoot, warble, yowl
DAY 1	WORD MEANING Write: *croak.* **What animals make a croaking sound?**
DAY 2 p. 94	RELATED WORDS Write: *croak, quack, caw.* **How are these words alike? What animals make these sounds?**
DAY 3 p. 95	ONOMATOPOEIA Write: *"Ribbit, ribbit," croak the frogs.* Ask volunteers to imitate the croaking sound of frogs.
DAY 4 p. 96	DESCRIPTIVE WORDS Read: *"My throat is sore,"* Jenny said. *"My throat is sore,"* Jenny croaked. **Which sentence is more descriptive? Why?**
DAY 5	SYNONYMS **Make a list of words you might use in your writing in place of the word *said.***

Chapter 35	WORDS OF THE WEEK: bolt, linger, dawdle, plunge, **scamper**
DAY 1	WORD MEANING Write: *Playful monkeys scamper about.* Discuss the meaning of *scamper.* (run quickly and lightly) **Do you think giraffes scamper?**
DAY 2 p. 103	SYNONYMS/ANTONYMS Write: *scamper, dash, stroll.* **Which words are synonyms? Which are antonyms?**
DAY 3 p. 104	COMPARE/CONTRAST Write: *scampering squirrel, dawdling snail.* **Which is faster?**
DAY 4 p. 105	CONTEXT CLUES Write: *We'll have to scamper to get this work done in time!* **What does *scamper* mean?**
DAY 5	TECHNOLOGY **Make a list of animals and words that describe the way they move.** Suggest that children use the computer to find information about the way various animals move.

Chapter 33	WORDS OF THE WEEK: **correspondence**, e-mail, memo, message, post
DAY 1	WORD MEANING Discuss the meaning of *correspondence.* (communicating by letters) **With whom might you have a *correspondence*?**
DAY 2 p. 97	RELATED WORDS List: *correspondence, letters, memo, message, post, notes.* **How are these words related?**
DAY 3 p. 98	CLIPPED WORDS List: *electronic mail, e-mail.* **How is the word *e-mail* like an abbreviation?**
DAY 4 p. 99	JARGON Write: *What is your e-mail address?* **Is your e-mail address the same as your street address? How is it different?**
DAY 5	TECHNOLOGY If possible, suggest that children correspond by writing each other e-mail messages about favorite books. Make a collection of their correspondence.

Chapter 36	WORDS OF THE WEEK: **recycled**, recount, rethink, retrace, review
DAY 1	WORD MEANING Write: *recycled.* **What does *recycled* mean?** (used over again) **What things do you recycle?**
DAY 2 p. 106	CONTEXT CLUES Write: *This newspaper will be recycled into grocery bags.* **What clues help you understand the meaning of *recycled*?**
DAY 3 p. 107	PREFIXES List: *cycle, recycle, use, reuse.* **Which are the base words? What has been added to *cycle* and *use* to make new words? What do the new words mean?**
DAY 4 p. 108	CONTENT-AREA WORDS Write: *Music, Art, Math.* **In which class would you recycle scrap paper to make a collage?**
DAY 5	FIGURATIVE LANGUAGE Discuss the meaning of the following: to *recycle* an idea, to *"reinvent* the wheel," to *rehash* a topic. Ask children to illustrate or give examples.

Activities

Word Wall

Create a Word Wall for children to use as a resource for reading, writing, and vocabulary development. Each week, add five or more words to the wall. These words can come from various sources: **Vocabulary Power** words, children's reading, or commonly misspelled words from children's writing. Write the words on cards and arrange them alphabetically. You may want to color-code the word cards. For example, use pink for nouns, yellow for verbs, and white for high-frequency words. Add each word to the Word Wall after it has been introduced. Continually add, take away, and move words around on the wall, as needed for instruction.

Word Wall Activities

- Have children regularly read all the words on the Word Wall.

- Have a word hunt. Ask children to look for categories of words, such as adjectives, plurals, or words with a common suffix. Categories can also be things like ways to move, baseball words, or math words.

- Say sentences with a blank for a missing word. Tell children the category of word that fits in the blank, such as a noun or a verb. Children choose words from the wall that fit the sentence.

- Dictate sentences using words from the Word Wall. Children can also create sentences with the words.

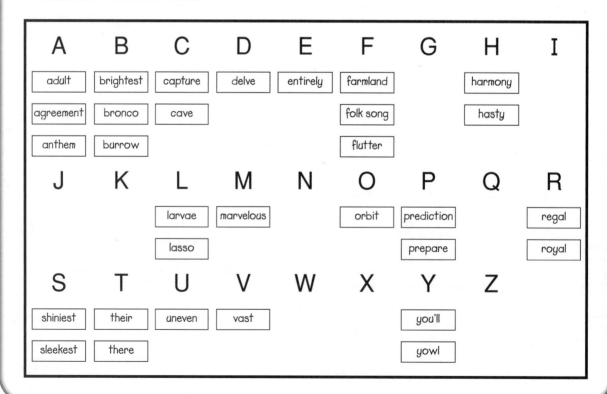

Journal

Children can record their **Vocabulary Power** words in a section in their journals. Have them record the words for each chapter on a page. Then they can do activities like these to extend their understanding of the words:

- illustrate the words
- write sentences or stories
- add more words that are related
- write synonyms and antonyms
- form plurals
- add endings to the words, such as *-ed* or *-ing*
- add other words that can be formed with the same base word

Chapter 1
capture
clutch
grab
grasp
seize

We captured a frog and then set it free.

Antonyms
release
let go

Say It!

To help children make the **Vocabulary Power** words part of their vocabulary, challenge them to use the words in everyday situations in the classroom. Make it fun! Encourage them to try out the new words. You may want to organize children into teams and have a chart or some other way to keep track of how often the words are used in a week.

I am eating a luscious lunch!

Act It Out!

Have a volunteer or small group choose a **Vocabulary Power** word to act out. The rest of the children guess the word. You can help children go beyond the **Vocabulary Power** words by having them act out related words also. Here is an example with the Vocabulary Power word *whirl*:

Make your body:

whirl	twirl	twist	swirl	coil
spin	curl	stretch	bend	droop
swing	turn	sway	lean	slouch

Word Cards

Vocabulary Power word cards can be found on pages T25–T39. Duplicate and distribute the cards. You may want to have children store the cards in a large self-seal baggy. They can write the meaning or an example sentence on the back of the card to help them learn the word. Children can use them as flash cards to read through and to quiz each other. The word cards can be glued onto index cards to add to the Word Wall. They can also be used in a variety of games.

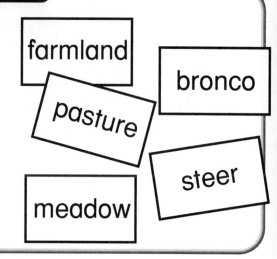

Concentration

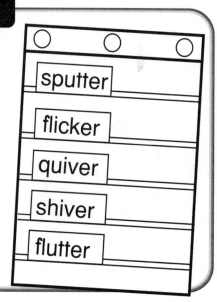

Have partners put their sets of word cards together face down. Each player takes a turn turning over two cards. If the cards match, the player keeps the cards and takes another turn. If the cards do not match, the cards are turned face down and the other player takes a turn.

Word Ladders

Put the words face down in a pile. Have a player choose a card, read it, and say the meaning or use it in a sentence. If it is correct, the word card is placed in the bottom pocket of a pocket chart or on a tabletop near the edge. The same player chooses another word and repeats the activity, placing the word above the other card. He or she tries to make as tall a ladder as possible. Challenge children to see who can make the tallest ladder and to read up and down each other's ladders.

Board Games

Make a simple path on a file folder or sheet of poster board. Write directions randomly on some of the spaces, such as *Take another turn* or *Leap ahead 2*. The player tosses a number cube or spins a spinner to find out how many spaces to move. The player picks a word card from the pile, reads the word, uses it in a sentence (or says a synonym, an antonym, and so on), and moves the number of spaces. He or she follows any directions on the space. Then the next player takes a turn. Generic gameboards can be used with different sets of word cards and directions to create a variety of fun games.

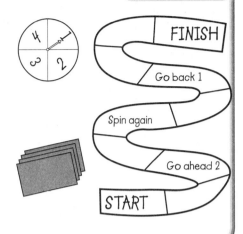

Word-o

Distribute a blank grid to each child. (A 16-square grid is good to use.) Display a list of words, and have children write them randomly in the squares. Children can use pieces of paper for markers or color the squares. The caller says the words randomly as children cover or color the appropriate square. A player who has a row covered down, across, or diagonally says, "Word-o!"

capture grab grasp anthem
folk song serenade
field totally jingle

Variations:
- Say the definition, and players mark the word.
- Say an antonym (or synonym), and players mark the word.
- Say an example sentence with a blank for the word, and players mark the word.

Word Searches

Children can make word-search puzzles by writing vocabulary words on graph paper (or similar paper), one letter to a box. Then they fill in the other boxes randomly with letters. At the bottom of the page, have them write a clue for each vocabulary word. Children can trade papers and circle the hidden words.

```
b  x  s  m  n  b  q  t  v  e
u  l  a  s  s  o  b  w  a  a
r  y  z  e  l  t  s  v  o  t
r  w  z  y  c  e  n  b  d  s
o  t  b  a  i  a  t  o  i  n
w  f  i  e  l  d  d  g  m  h
```
1. grassy area   2. caterpillars
3. cowboy's rope 4. animal's home

Spinning for Words

Cut out a large cardboard circle and section it off into eight pie-shaped slices. Write a word, such as an antonym, and a number on each slice. (See the word lists on pages T19–T24.) Write the corresponding number and antonym on the back of each slice. Attach a spinning arrow to the wheel. Invite a volunteer to be a contestant on the "Spinning for Words" game show. Have the volunteer spin the spinner and read the word. The volunteer then says the antonym for that word and turns the wheel over to check. Permit contestants to ask for help from the audience as needed.

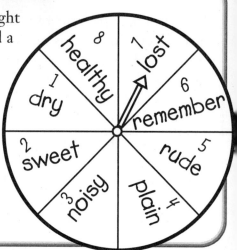

Mystery Word

On the board, write a word that has a synonym, such as *all*. Next to it, draw blank lines—one line for each of the letters in the synonym (*every*). Tell children that the word *all* has a mystery synonym that has five letters. Invite them to guess letters as you record the correct guesses in the blanks. Make a list of the incorrect guesses so that children won't choose those letters again. This game can be adapted for use with antonyms, **Vocabulary Power** words that are related by topic, and so on. (See the word lists on pages T19–T24 for synonyms and other kinds of words to use.)

Synonym Snowballs

Cut some white circles to form snowballs and white igloo shapes to form snow forts. Write a synonym on each snowball. (See the word list on page T19 for examples.) In small groups, have children lay the snowballs face down on the floor. Each player gets a snow fort. Players should take turns choosing two snowballs, reading the words, and deciding if the words are synonyms. If they are synonyms, children should keep the snowball pair in the fort. The game continues until all snowball pairs are in a fort. This game can be adapted for use with **Vocabulary Power** words, antonyms, and so on.

Graphic Organizers

Graphic organizers are powerful thinking tools. They can help children organize information they gather during reading, listening, and learning new vocabulary. Graphic organizers provide conceptual frames in which children can collect and categorize ideas. Within those frames, children can see relationships and make connections. As children use these thinking tools, they will begin to see the recurring relationships and connections that exist among words and concepts.

Semantic Mapping

Semantic mapping is a concept development approach to vocabulary instruction. It shows children the organization and relationship of concepts in a visual way.

Semantic mapping involves three steps:
1. **Brainstorm** and list words related to a concept or topic.
2. **Classify** ideas to decide what categories seem to be represented.
3. **Map** the information to visually represent the relationship between the ideas. Add labels to the map to further the classification practice.

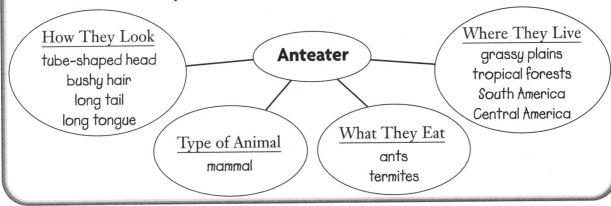

Word Web

Word Webs are collections of related words. Using a center space and web strands, children generate structurally or conceptually related words.

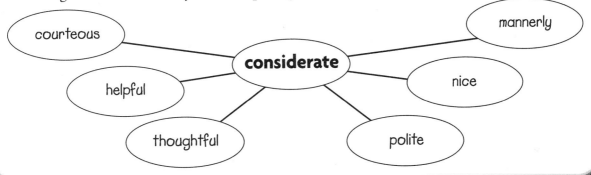

Shape Summary

The Shape Summary is useful in making comparisons between more than one word or concept.

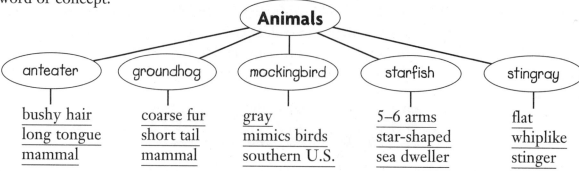

Animals

anteater	groundhog	mockingbird	starfish	stingray
bushy hair	coarse fur	gray	5–6 arms	flat
long tongue	short tail	mimics birds	star-shaped	whiplike
mammal	mammal	southern U.S.	sea dweller	stinger

Venn Diagram

The Venn Diagram is used with words and ideas to show features in common between two different concepts.

Cave
stone
formed by nature

animal home
has an opening
hollow

Burrow
soil
made by animal

Word Square

The Word Square requires children to recall a word definition, visualize the definition, and describe what the word is not. This graphic is particularly helpful to English language learners.

1. field	2.
3. an open land area without trees or buildings	4. Not

Word Lists

Antonyms

Antonyms are words with opposite meanings.

above — below	far — near	lost — found
add — subtract	finish — begin	more — less
after — before	first — last	neat — messy
alone — together	float — sink	noisy — quiet
answer — question	give — take	nothing — everything
awake — asleep	healthy — sick	plain — fancy
back — front	high — low	remember — forget
big — little	hot — cold	rude — polite
bottom — top	in — out	sweet — sour
dry — wet	lend — borrow	tall — short
easy — difficult	long — short	

Synonyms

Synonyms are words with the same, or nearly the same meanings.

all — every	end — finish	press — squeeze
amaze — surprise	fast — quick	shout — yell
answer — response	fix — repair	shut — close
back — rear	happy — joyful	sleepy — drowsy
big — large	high — tall	start — begin
bother — pester	huge — enormous	under — below
buddy — friend	look — peek	
children — kids	loud — noisy	

Homophones

Homophones are words that sound the same but have different meanings and usually have different spellings.

ant — aunt	for — four	peace — piece
ate — eight	heal — heel	right — write
be — bee	hi — high	road — rode — rowed
beach — beech	hoarse — horse	sail — sale
beat — beet	hole — whole	sea — see
berry — bury	I — eye	son — sun
blew — blue	meat — meet	stair — stare
brake — break	new — knew	their — there — they're
cent — sent	no — know	to — too — two
close — clothes	oar — or	wail — whale
dear — deer	one — won	weak — week
flew — flu	pail — pale	we'll — wheel
flour — flower	pair — pear	wood — would

Homographs

Homographs are words that are spelled the same but have different meanings and different origins (*bat* the mammal, *bat* the club). Some homographs also have different pronunciations (*august* majestic, *August* eighth month).

close — shut / near

dove — pigeon / did dive

live — to exist / having life

desert — abandon / arid land

object — thing / disagree

record — to make note of / best achievement

tear — rip / drop of water from an eye

refuse — to say no / trash

lead — heavy metal / to be first

does — form of do / female deer

Prefixes

Prefixes are letter groups added before a base word to change or add to the word's meaning.

Prefix	Meaning	Example
auto-	self	autobiography
bi-	two	bicycle, biweekly
dis-	not	disbelief
im-	not	impossible
in-	into, not	inside, independence
non-	not	nonfiction
pre-	before	prehistoric
re-	again	resend
tele-	far	telescope
trans-	across	transportation
tri-	three	triangle
uni-	one	unify

Suffixes

Suffixes are letter groups added after a base word to change or add to the word's meaning.

Suffix	Meaning	Example
-er	one who	teacher
-er	more	brighter
-est	most	brightest
-ful	full of	wonderful
-ing	(present tense)	smiling
-less	without	penniless
-ling	small	duckling
-ly	every	weekly
-ly	(adverb)	quickly
-ness	state of being	happiness
-or	one who	actor
-y	state of	funny

Words for Said

added	chimed in	insisted	promised	scolded
admitted	cried	interrupted	questioned	screamed
agreed	exclaimed	joked	reasoned	shouted
answered	explained	mentioned	recalled	snapped
argued	gasped	moaned	rejoiced	spoke
asked	groaned	murmured	reminded	stammered
babbled	growled	muttered	repeated	stated
begged	grumbled	noted	replied	teased
bellowed	grunted	ordered	requested	told
blurted out	guessed	pleaded	responded	whispered
boasted	hinted	pointed out	roared	yelled
bragged	inquired	praised	sang	

Words for Went

ambled	flowed	skated
bounced	galloped	skipped
chased	hopped	slid
climbed	hurried	sped
crawled	marched	stepped
crept	moved	traveled
danced	ran	trotted
drove	rode	walked
flew	rushed	
floated	sailed	

Clipped Words

These words are shortened forms of words that are easier to say and use.

ad — advertisement
bike — bicycle
cab — cabriolet
champ — champion
exam — examination
fan — fanatic
gas — gasoline
flu — influenza

gym — gymnasium
lab — laboratory
lunch — luncheon
math — mathematics
phone — telephone
plane — airplane
ref — referee
taxi — taxicab

Onomatopoeic Words

Onomatopoeic words sound like their meanings.

bark
boom
buzz
chirp
clack
clang
click
clink
clomp
cluck
coo

crackle
fizz
hiss
moo
oink
plink
plop
pop
quack
screech
slurp

splash
swish
thud
tick
whiz
zap
zoom

Portmanteau Words

Portmanteau words are two words that have been blended into one.

brunch — breakfast and lunch
clash — clap and crash
o'clock — of the clock

smash — smack and mash
smog — smoke and fog
squiggle — squirm and wiggle

Descriptive Words

balmy	flat	noisy	spicy
bitter	fluffy	nutty	splash
breezy	foggy	quiet	sticky
bright	fresh	rotten	straight
clear	frigid	rough	sweet
cold	fuzzy	round	tall
colorful	gooey	salty	tangy
cool	gritty	sharp	thump
creaky	hot	shrill	thundering
crinkled	huge	silent	tight
dark	light	slick	tiny
delicious	long	slimy	wet
dry	loud	slippery	
enormous	low	snarl	
faint	muddy	sour	

capture	clutch
grab	grasp
seize	anthem
folk song	jingle
lullaby	serenade
burrow	cave

lair	lodge
roost	entirely
mostly	partly
totally	wholly
agreement	disagreement
disharmony	harmony

togetherness	brightest
glossiest	shiniest
sleekest	smoothest
countryside	farmland
field	meadow
pasture	adult

cocoons	cycle
larvae	pupa
bronco	lasso
rodeo	saddle
steer	ambassador
chairperson	mayor

officer	president
cattail	cowhand
pigtail	rattlesnake
turtleneck	delve
explored	inquire
observe	quest

flicker	flutter
quiver	shiver
sputter	communicate
confer	consulting
converse	recommend
category	family

similar	species
specimen	circular
orbit	revolving
spinning	spiral
anchored	attached
connected	fastened

united	beasts
beings	creatures
critters	varmints
considerate	courteous
mannerly	polite
thoughtful	appetizing

delicious	flavorful
luscious	savory
coil	swirl
twirl	twist
whirl	countless
endless	infinite

unlimited	vast
hasty	quicker
rapid	speedily
swiftest	dignified
formal	noble
regal	royal

action	connection
contribution	prediction
transportation	frayed
ragged	shaggy
tattered	uneven
demonstrate	display

illustrate	model
present	advise
direct	guided
led	taught
angrily	gracefully
hungrily	noisily

playfully	interact
intercom	interleaf
international	Internet
anteater	groundhog
mockingbird	starfish
stingray	bellow

croak	hoot
warble	yowl
correspondence	e-mail
memo	message
post	fabulous
fantastic	marvelous

splendid	superb
bolt	linger
dawdle	plunge
scamper	recycled
recount	rethink
retrace	review

Vocabulary Power

GRADE 2

Printed in the United States of America

ISBN 0-15-320608-X

4 5 6 7 8 9 10 082 2003 2002

Table of Contents

CHAPTER

CHAPTER

Name _____

<u>Synonyms</u> are words that have similar meanings.

small–little–tiny   jump–leap–hop   cry–sob–weep

The word <u>seize</u> has many synonyms. Read the words in the box.
Circle the four words that mean the same or almost the same
as <u>seize</u>.

grab	**forget**	**drop**	**capture**
lose	**clutch**	**grasp**	**shout**

Draw a picture to show the meaning of each action.

grab	**capture**
clutch	**grasp**

Name _____

Endings can be added to base words to make new words.

| help | pitch | stop | like | run | make |
| helps | pitches | stopped | liked | running | making |

Fill in the chart to make new words.

Base Word	Add -s or -es	Add -ed	Add -ing
grasp	grasps	grasped	grasping
clutch	clutches	clutched	clutching
grab	grabs	grabbed	grabbing
seize	seizes	seized	seizing
capture	captures	captured	capturing

Choose one of the words you wrote in the chart. Draw a picture and write a sentence using the word.

Responses will vary.

Name _____

What does this saying mean? | Put on your thinking cap.

You can't wear a <u>thinking cap</u>. The saying means "to think hard about something."

What does this saying mean? | Seize the day!

When you "seize the day," you use the day to do many different things.

	It's lunchtime. Let's <u>grab a bite</u>.
It's time to put on your thinking cap. Draw a picture to show the meaning of the underlined words.	
I'm learning how to use a map. I can <u>grasp the idea</u>.	I'm in a play. I act sad. I can <u>capture the feeling</u>.

Context clues can help you understand the meaning of new words.

Grandpa sang a <u>lullaby</u> to the baby. The baby soon fell asleep.

What kind of song is a <u>lullaby</u>? Fast and loud or slow and soothing? Underline the words that help you understand that a <u>lullaby</u> is slow and soothing.

Use the clues to help you understand the meaning of the underlined words. Circle the letter beside the correct meaning.

1. When we sing our country's <u>anthem</u>, we stand up.
An <u>anthem</u> is a song _____.
A of praise
B that is slow and sad
C with a good beat

2. My mom wrote a <u>jingle</u> for Poppy Popcorn.
A <u>jingle</u> is a song _____.
A for bells
B for dancing
C to sell something

3. My grandmother learned this <u>folk song</u> from her grandmother.
A <u>folk song</u> is _____.
A about grandparents
B about folks
C very old

4. On Valentine's Day, Dad stood outside and sang a <u>serenade</u> to Mom.
A <u>serenade</u> is a song _____.
A about hearts
B sung to someone
C that only fathers can sing

Name _____

Words, ideas, objects, and pictures can be grouped together.

PETS: cat, dog, fish, bird   FRUIT: banana, orange, plum, pear

Circle the words in the box that name a kind of song.

piano	jingle	folk	lullaby
anthem	green	saw	serenade

Complete each box. Write the names of things that belong in each group. You can use words from the box above.

KINDS OF SONGS	COLORS
MUSICAL INSTRUMENTS	**TOOLS**

Name _____

The words in the box are related because they name kinds of songs—but each kind of song is different from the others.

lullaby	jingle
serenade	anthem
folk song	

Draw pictures about different kinds of songs. For example, a picture for "lullaby" would not show people dancing and clapping their hands. Choose songs from the box above or think of other kinds of songs. Label each picture.

Responses will vary.

Vocabulary Power

Name _____

Context means "the way in which a word is used." What context clues help you understand the meaning of the underlined word?

Some animals dig underground homes called burrows.

The words animals, dig, and underground homes help you understand that burrows are "underground homes."

Answer each question by circling the letter beside the best answer.

1. The mother fox takes food to her babies in their safe lair. What clues help you understand that a lair is a home?

   A the, to, her   **B** food, babies, safe

2. All those birds have a roost in that little birdhouse. What clues help you understand that birds perch in a roost?

   A all, that, little   **B** birds, birdhouse

3. The beavers used sticks, twigs, and leaves to build their lodge. What clues help you understand how beavers make a lodge?

   A sticks, twigs, leaves, build   **B** used, and, leaves

4. The opening in the side of the hill leads to a bear's cave. What clues help you understand that a cave is underground?

   A opening, side of the hill   **B** side, leads to a

Name _____

Many words have more than one meaning.

An animal's underground home is called a <u>burrow</u>.
I'm going to <u>burrow</u> under the blanket to get warm.

All of the underlined words can name animal homes. Draw a picture to show another meaning for each underlined word.

1. I'm so tired! Let's stop and <u>roost</u> on this bench.	**2.** Joe cleared the snow off the roof. He was afraid the roof might <u>cave</u> in.
3. The pirates hid the stolen treasure in their secret <u>lair</u>. No one could find it.	**4.** When we went to the beach, we stayed at the Seaside <u>Lodge</u>.

Name _____

The words in the box name different kinds of homes. Use these words when you follow the directions in boxes 1 and 2 below.

cottage	lair	apartment	lodge	house
burrow	cave	roost	cabin	tent

1. ANIMALS' HOMES

You would learn about animals' homes in Science class. List animals' homes here.

2. PEOPLE'S HOMES

You would learn about people's homes in Social Studies class. List people's homes here.

3. OTHER SCIENCE WORDS

Write some other Science words you know.

4. OTHER SOCIAL STUDIES WORDS

Write some other Social Studies words you know.

Related Words are alike in some way. The words *whole* and *wholly* are related because of the base word whole.	whole + -ly = wholly The whole sky is not blue. The sky is not wholly blue.
Words can also be related by meaning. Draw a circle around the two words that mean the same as wholly. Draw a box around the two words that describe parts of a whole.	totally entirely mostly partly

Draw pictures to show the meaning of the underlined words:

mostly red	totally yellow
entirely green	partly pink

Name _____

Words that have the same base word are part of
the same <u>word family</u>.

whole
wholly

     whole + ly = wholly

Add -ly to these words:

entire + ly = _____ entirely   total + ly = _____ totally

most + ly = _____ mostly   part + ly = _____ partly

Draw a picture to show the meaning of the underlined word.

full + ly = <u>fully</u>	entire + ly = <u>entirely</u>
one + ly = <u>only</u>	part + ly = <u>partly</u>

Name _____

<u>Homophones</u> are words that sound the same.

The words <u>whole</u> and <u>hole</u> sound the same.

Are the words <u>whole</u> and <u>hole</u> spelled the same?
Do the words <u>whole</u> and <u>hole</u> have the same meaning?

What about the following underlined words? Write <u>YES</u> or <u>NO</u>.

The sky is not <u>wholly</u> blue.   Swiss Cheese is <u>holey</u>.

Do <u>wholly</u> and <u>holey</u> sound the same?   _____YES_____

Are <u>wholly</u> and <u>holey</u> spelled the same?   _____NO_____

Do <u>wholly</u> and <u>holey</u> mean the same?   _____NO_____

The following words are homophones. Circle one of the words. Draw a picture to show the meaning of the word you circled.

pair–pear	**to–too–two**
ate–eight	**red–read**

Name _____

Some words have the same or almost the same meanings. Other words have opposite meanings.

<u>same meanings:</u> little, small
<u>opposite meanings:</u> small, large

Which words mean the same as the word in dark print? Which mean the opposite? Write the words in the correct box.

harmony   agreement   disagreement
                 disharmony   togetherness

Same meaning as <u>harmony</u>	Opposite of <u>harmony</u>

Draw a picture to show the meaning of the sentences.

We are working together. We're in <u>agreement</u>. We are in <u>harmony</u>.	We are working together. We're having a <u>disagreement</u>. We are in <u>disharmony</u>.

Adding a beginning or an ending to a base word can change the meaning.

    dis + harmony = disharmony
    together + ness = togetherness

Add dis- to the beginning of these words to make new words.	**Choose one word and draw a picture to show its meaning.**
agreement _disagreement_	
please _displease_	
appear _disappear_	
color _discolor_	
continue _discontinue_	
Add -ness to the end of these words to make new words.	**Choose one word and draw a picture to show its meaning.**
together _togetherness_	
bright _brightness_	
silly _silliness_	
dark _darkness_	
fresh _freshness_	

Some words are related by meaning. The following words are related because they all have something to do with <u>music</u>.

sing   harmony   melody

Circle the words in the box that are related to <u>music</u>.

band	singer	garden	lyrics	piano
boat	telephone	tune	dance	lunchbox

These words are related because they all have something to do with <u>friendship</u>.

togetherness   talk   play   understanding

Write some other related words. Draw a picture about <u>friendship</u>.

Words that have the same base word are in the same word family.

glossy   glossier   glossiest

Add -er and -est to these words to make word families.

bright   **shiny**

brighter   shinier
_____   _____

brightest   shiniest
_____   _____

sleek   **smooth**

sleeker   smoother
_____   _____

sleekest   smoothest
_____   _____

Draw pictures to show the meaning of the underlined words.

the brightest object in the sky	the sleekest fur of all
the shiniest shoes in the store	the smoothest ice cream ever

Name _____

The words glossier and glossiest can be used to compare things.

My cat has glossier fur than your cat.
My cat has the glossiest fur of all the cats.

Add -er or -est to the word in dark print. Write the word that best completes the sentence.

shiny   **1.** That star is the _____ shiniest _____ star in the sky.

smooth   **2.** Apples feel _____ smoother _____ than oranges.

sleek   **3.** Cheetahs are _____ sleeker _____ than hippos.

bumpy   **4.** This is the _____ bumpiest _____ road in town.

funny   **5.** Barb's joke was _____ funnier _____ than mine.

tasty   **6.** I think popcorn is the _____ tastiest _____ treat.

Complete and draw a picture for each sentence.

_____ is brighter than _____ .	_____ is the brightest.

Name _____

Some words can be used in many different ways. Read these sentences. Think about the meanings of the underlined words.

The glossiest shoes are the shiniest of all.
We are going to paint the room with gloss paint.

Gloss paint is a kind of paint that is shiny when it dries.

Circle the meaning of each underlined word.

1. Raj is the brightest boy in math class.
shiniest
sunniest
(smartest)

2. Bonnie has the smoothest manners of anyone I know.
(most polite)
least lumpy
flattest

3. Ali shines in art class.
sparks
(does well)
becomes glossy

4. Tom has a bright smile.
sleek
(happy)
sun-shaped

Lights can shine, beam, glow, or sparkle. Draw a picture to show how people can do the same.

Name _____

You would probably find all of these words in a book about
the sea.

salt   water   fish   waves   tides   shells   shore

Think about the words you might find in a book about farms.
Fill in the word web below. Use words from the box. Add
other words.

field	sidewalk	pasture	farmland	skyscraper
desk	airport	meadow	gym	countryside

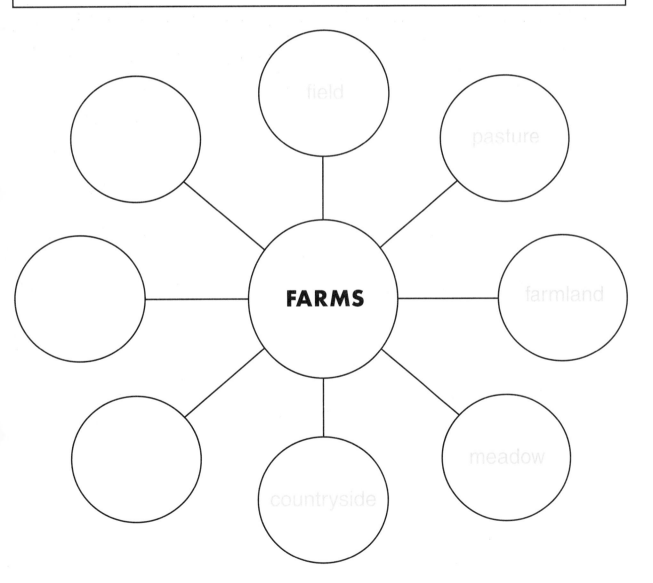

Name_____

A compound word is made by putting two words together.

country + side = countryside

Join the word in dark print with the other words. In the last box, draw and label a picture for one of the words you wrote.

side in out walk	**yard** back farm stick
inside	backyard
outside	farmyard
sidewalk	yardstick
land grass dream mark	**house** hen farm boat
grassland	henhouse
dreamland	farmhouse
landmark	houseboat/boathouse
field corn ball work	
cornfield	
ballfield	
fieldwork	

Vocabulary Power

Name _____

Look at each word puzzle. Think about why the words go together.

big—large	up—down	round—ball
hot—warm	city—country	square—box

<u>Big</u> and <u>large</u> have similar meanings. Why does <u>warm</u> belong with <u>hot</u>?

<u>Up</u> and <u>down</u> are opposites. Why does <u>country</u> belong with <u>city</u>?
A <u>ball</u> is <u>round</u>. Why does <u>box</u> belong with <u>square</u>?

Complete the word puzzles. Think about why the first two words go together. Write a word that goes with the third word in the same way. Use the words in the box to help you.

gardener	**cow**	**sad**	**small**	**bird**	**sand**

1. shiny — bright

little — _____

2. no — yes

happy — _____

3. kitten — cat

calf — _____

4. farm — farmer

garden — _____

5. pasture — grass

desert — _____

6. gallop — horse

fly — _____

Name _____

Read the following science article. Think about the meaning of the underlined words.

The Life of the Butterfly

Butterflies start out as eggs. The eggs hatch into caterpillars, or larvae. Caterpillars eat and grow quickly. Then they make shells, or cocoons.

Inside its cocoon, the caterpillar is called a pupa. The pupa grows, changes, and becomes an adult.

When the cocoon cracks open, out comes a butterfly! The butterfly lays eggs, and the cycle begins again.

Moths have a life cycle similar to butterflies. Use what you learned about butterflies to tell about moths.

Moth eggs hatch into caterpillars, or _____larvae_____.

The caterpillars wrap themselves in _____cocoons_____.

Inside a cocoon, a caterpillar is called a _____pupa_____.

The pupa grows into an _____adult_____.

When the cocoon cracks open, out comes a moth.

The moth lays eggs, and the _____cycle_____ begins again.

Name _____

Related Words

Words can be related in many different ways.

These are stages in the life of a moth: cocoon, pupa, adult.
These are different kinds of birds: robin, cardinal, woodpecker.
These are games you play with a ball: football, basketball,
baseball.

**Brainstorm words that are related in some way to the words in
dark print. Tell how your words are related.**

baby	shell
_____	_____
_____	_____
_____	_____
These words are related because	These words are related because
_____.	_____.
cycle	**butterfly**
_____	_____
_____	_____
_____	_____
These words are related because	These words are related because
_____.	_____.

Vocabulary Power

Name _____

Each word pair belongs in the same word family. The first word names "one," and the second word names "more than one."

| cocoon | fox | fish | pupa | tooth |
| cocoon<u>s</u> | fox<u>es</u> | fish | pup<u>ae</u> | teeth |

Complete each phrase. Then draw a picture for your phrase.

1. one <u>mouse</u> in a <u>burrow</u>

six _____mice_____ in

two _____burrows_____

2. one <u>caterpillar</u>, one <u>larva</u>

two _____caterpillars_____,

two _____larvae_____

3. one <u>sheep</u> on a <u>hill</u>

four _____sheep_____ on

two _____hills_____

4. one <u>child</u> standing on one <u>foot</u>

two _____children_____ standing on

two _____feet_____

Name _____

Context clues can help you figure out word meanings. What words help you understand what a <u>rodeo</u> is?

At the <u>rodeo</u> we saw people riding horses and doing lots of tricks. It was a great show!

Here are more sentences about the rodeo. Draw a picture. Include the underlined words in your picture.

The brown <u>bronco</u> was the wildest horse of all. The rider started out sitting in the <u>saddle</u>, but he soon ended up on the ground!

One rider did tricks with a rope. She swung her <u>lasso</u> in the air. The loop landed around the horns of a <u>steer</u>.

Many English words come from words in other languages. These words come from the Spanish language of Mexico. Which word names a snack you might have at a rodeo? Circle the word.

rodeo   bronco   lasso   (nachos)

The names of many foods come from other languages. Circle the names of the foods you have eaten.

bagel	taco	pizza
baklava	goulash	ravioli
burrito	knish	spaghetti
chili	mousse	succotash
chow mein	pierogi	tortilla

Draw and label some of your favorite foods. Use a dictionary to find out if the names come from a language other than English.

Name _____

Words can be grouped together because they name things that belong in the same category.

COLORS: red, gray, green   EXERCISES: push-ups, jumping-jacks

Write words from the box under RODEO or CIRCUS.

bronco-riding	tumblers	steer-roping
tightrope walkers	lasso tricks	juggling

RODEO	CIRCUS
bronco-riding	tumblers
steer-roping	tightrope walkers
lasso tricks	juggling

Write the names of things that belong in these categories.

TELEVISION SHOWS	ANIMAL SOUNDS

Vocabulary Power

Name _____

Many people work for the government. These workers often have special titles. Being an <u>ambassador</u> is an important job.

One country sends an <u>ambassador</u> to another country.
The <u>ambassador</u> helps the two countries exchange ideas.

Match these titles with the jobs.

officer	president	chairperson	mayor

1. The leader of a city is a _____.

2. A member of the police force is a police _____.

3. The leader of a country is a _____.

4. Someone in charge of a meeting is a _____.

Which job would you like to have? Draw a picture and write about why you would like the job.

Vocabulary Power

Name _____

An abbreviation is a short form of a word. It usually begins with a capital letter and ends with a period. An abbreviation comes from letters in the word.

Ambassador Ying lives on Spencer Avenue.
Amb.   Ying lives on Spencer Ave.

Complete each person's name by writing an abbreviation. Use the underlined letters in the word in dark print. (Don't forget the capital letter and the period.)

president   **1.** Here's a picture of _____ Grant.

officer   **2.** I think _____ Jake is in charge of traffic.

captain   **3.** The owner of the boat is _____ Hakel.

general   **4.** My aunt is in the army. She is _____ Beller.

professor   **5.** In college, my history teacher was _____ Gomez.

Complete each place name by writing an abbreviation. Use the underlined letters in the word in dark print.

university   **6.** My mom works at the _____ of Texas.

saint   **7.** That huge building is _____ Mary's Hospital.

route   **8.** This highway is called _____ 95.

Name _____

You don't have to work for the government to be an <u>ambassador</u>. These sentences tell about another kind of <u>ambassador</u>.

Erin is an <u>ambassador</u> for the local animal shelter.
Donald is an <u>ambassador</u> for healthy eating.

What kind of <u>ambassador</u> would you like to be? Think about something important to you. Draw and write about your ideas.

You can also be a <u>president</u>. Start a club. You can be <u>president</u> of your club. Draw and write about your ideas.

You can be a <u>chairperson</u>. Hold a meeting. Lead the meeting. Draw and write about yourself being a <u>chairperson</u>.

Vocabulary Power

Name _____

A compound word is made by joining two words together. Some compound words mean exactly what they say.

rattle + snake = rattlesnake
A <u>rattlesnake</u> is a snake that makes a rattling sound.

Some compound words can fool you. Join these words together to make compound words.

1. cat + tail = _____

2. cow + hand = _____

3. pig + tail = _____

4. turtle + neck = _____

Circle the meaning of each compound word.

5. What is a <u>pigtail</u>?   a pig's curly tail
                     braided hair

6. What is a <u>cowhand</u>?   a cow-shaped hand
                      someone who works with cattle

7. What is a <u>turtleneck</u>?   a collar decorated with turtles
                      a high collar

8. What is a <u>cattail</u>?   a cat's long, fluffy tail
                    a plant whose flowers look like a cat's tail

These compound words belong to the same word family. Underline the word that appears in each compound word.

rattle<u>snake</u>   <u>snake</u>weed   <u>snake</u>bite   black<u>snake</u>

Make compound words. The word in dark print should be in each compound word.

1. cat nip fish bear	**2. tail** pig gate spin
___catnip___	___pigtail___
___catfish___	___tailgate___
___bearcat___	___tailspin___
3. hand cow shake book	**4. neck** turtle band tie
___cowhand___	___turtleneck___
___handshake___	___neckband___
___handbook___	___necktie___
5. bird yellow call seed	**6. house** tree fly plant
___yellowbird___	___treehouse___
___birdcall___	___housefly___
___birdseed___	___houseplant___

Name _____

Some words describe sounds. A <u>rattlesnake</u> got its name because of the sound it makes when it's getting ready to strike.

Read the sound word. Write the name of an animal that makes the sound.

1. meow _____

2. hoot _____

3. cluck _____

4. roar _____

5. growl _____

6. croak _____

7. squeal _____

8. buzz _____

Other words name sounds in nature. Draw pictures to show what could make the following sounds.

drip-drip-drop	**whoosh**
crack! boom!	**ker-plop!**

Many words are related by meaning. The first two words are related because they have similar meanings. The third word is related because it names something someone would look for.

explored—searched—treasure

Read the words in the box. They are related to the word <u>explore</u>.

inquire	**observe**	**delve**	**quest**

Read the related words. Think about things you would like to learn about, such as an animal, the stars, or how to do something. Write or draw the answer to each question.

1. inquire—ask—question What would you like to <u>inquire</u> about?	**2.** observe—watch—follow What would you like to <u>observe</u>?
3. delve—mystery—seek What would you like to <u>delve</u> into?	**4.** quest—searching—travel Where would you like to go on a <u>quest</u>?

Name _____

The following words are in the same word family. They each have the same base word—<u>search</u>.

search + -ing = <u>searching</u>   search + -ed = <u>searched</u>
search + re- = <u>research</u>   research + -er = <u>researcher</u>

Use the base words to make new words. (Remember: For some words, you have to drop the final <u>e</u> before adding an ending.)

1. quest Add -ion, re-. question _____ request _____	**2. explore** Add -ing, -er. exploring _____ explorer _____
3. delve Add -ed, -ing. delved _____ delving _____	**4. inquire** Add -ed, -ing. inquired _____ inquiring _____
5. observe Add -s, -er, -ation. observes _____ observer _____ observation _____	**6. examine** Add -ed, -er, -ation. examined _____ examiner _____ examination _____

Name _____

There are many ways to explore. Some explorers travel far to find dinosaur bones. Some explorers dive into the ocean to study sea creatures. Not everyone can travel far or dive into the ocean—but everyone can be an explorer.

Read the questions to help you brainstorm ideas.

How could you explore life in the desert?

How could you observe wildlife?

How could you inquire about how to publish a newspaper?

How could you delve into the world of sharks?

Draw and write about ways you can be an explorer. Share your ideas.

Responses will vary.

Name_____

These words are related because they describe ways to move.

swim   float   dive

The words in dark print describe other ways to move. Draw pictures to show the word meanings. For number 6, write and draw about your own word.

1. flutter	**2.** flicker
3. shiver	**4.** quiver
5. sputter	**6.** _____

Vocabulary Power

Name _____

Many words have more than one meaning. Read these sentences.

A. The lightning bolts flash.   **B.** I'll be back in a flash.

In **A** flash means "to blaze quickly." In **B** flash means "a very short amount of time."

Read the sentence pairs. Draw a picture of yourself to show the meaning of the sentence in dark print.

I. The candlelight can flicker. **I just felt a flicker of a chill.**	**2.** Butterflies flutter to and fro. **My stomach is starting to flutter.**
3. The leaves shiver in the breeze. **Cold weather makes me shiver.**	**4.** The fire will soon sputter and die. **I'm so happy, I'm starting to sputter.**

Vocabulary Power

Some rhyming words have similar meanings. Most don't. Circle the words that rhyme and have a similar meaning.

float—coat   shake—quake   tickle—pickle

Write rhyming words for the word in dark print. Draw and label a picture for one of the rhyming words.

flutter _____	**flicker** _____
_____ _____	_____ _____
quiver _____	**flash** _____
_____ _____	_____ _____

Name _____

Synonyms have similar meanings. The following words are synonyms.

talk—speak   trade—exchange   send—transmit

Think about the meaning of the underlined word. Choose and write the word that has a similar meaning.

1. The nurse is <u>consulting</u> the doctor.

agreeing   asking   writing   _asking_ _____

2. My friend and I <u>converse</u> by phone.

speak   giggle   explore   _speak_ _____

3. My parents <u>confer</u> with my teacher.

travel   instruct   meet   _meet_ _____

4. I <u>recommend</u> that you read this book.

advise   order   understand   _advise_ _____

5. Writing is one way to <u>communicate</u> ideas.

forget   observe   express   _express_ _____

Draw pictures to show different ways to <u>communicate</u>.

Name _____

The following words belong to the same word family. Underline the base word in each.

consulting   consultant   consultation

1. Write the base word at the top of each word ladder.

confer	converse
conferred	converses
conferring	conversing
conference	conversation
recommend	communicate
recommended	communicates
recommending	communicating
recommendation	communication

2. Get together with some classmates. Have a conference. Converse about your favorite books. Ask each other to make recommendations. Draw a picture to show how you and your friends communicated.

An abbreviation is a short way to write a word.

    Street—St.   August—Aug.   President—Pres.

Write the abbreviations. Then answer the questions. Write or draw or do both. Share your ideas with classmates.

---

1. _____ Prof. _____ Ed James is an expert on space and space travel.
Professor
If you could confer with an expert on space, what would you ask?

---

2. _____ Pres. _____ George Washington was born in 1732.
President
If you could have a conversation with George Washington, what would you talk about?

---

3. _____ Dr. _____ Fritz works at _____ Mt. _____ J. Animal Hospital.
Doctor   Mount
How do you think an animal doctor communicates with animals?

Name _____

The following words have special meanings in science. The words are used to tell about all living things.

category   family   similar   species   specimen

This chart shows how scientists use these words.
What animal is the chart about? Fill in the last box.

KINGDOM	Animal
CLASS	**Mammal** (warm-blooded, has hair or fur)
ORDER	**Carnivore** (eats meat)
FAMILY	**Cat** (includes cats of all sizes)
SPECIES	Tiger

- Each <u>category</u> in the chart tells about the tiger.
- The tiger is <u>similar</u> to other animals in many ways.
- The cat <u>family</u> is very large. The tiger is one <u>species</u> of cat.
- To see a <u>specimen</u>, you have to visit a zoo. A <u>specimen</u> is "one."

What other species do you think belong to the cat family? Draw and label a specimen. How is your cat similar to a tiger?

Name _____

Some words have special scientific meanings, but they also have everyday meanings.

My kitten Jingles is a member of the cat <u>family</u>.
Jingles is also a member of my <u>family</u>!

Complete the sentences. Share your ideas with classmates.

1. My friend and I have <u>similar</u> _____.

2. That _____ is a sad <u>specimen</u>!

3. These things belong in the "_____" <u>category</u>.

4. The _____ is so good that it must be a special <u>species</u>!

Draw and label pictures for two of the sentences above.

Vocabulary Power

Look at the following word puzzles. Think about how the first two words go together. What one word completes each puzzle?

roar–tiger   puppy–dog   birds–bird

meow–_____   kitten–_____   cats–_____

Complete these word puzzles. Remember to think about how the first two words go together.

1. moon–night sun–_____	**2.** mittens–hands boots–_____
3. similar–different down–_____	**4.** doctor–Dr. street–_____
5. mouse–mice tooth–_____	**6.** category–group glad–_____
7. nose–smell eyes–_____	**8.** hard–soft rough–_____
9. prince–princess king–_____	**10.** fish–scales bear–_____

Make up two word puzzles on another sheet of paper. Ask a classmate to complete them.

What word in this sentence helps you understand the meaning of revolving?

    The Earth is revolving around the sun.

The word around helps you understand that revolving means "going around."

The word around can help you understand the meaning of other words. Read each sentence. Draw a picture to show the meaning of the underlined word.

I. The moon's path around the Earth is called an orbit.	**2.** The dancer is spinning around on one foot!
3. We walked around in a circular path.	**4.** If I twist a string around my finger, I can make a spiral.

Name _____

A word family is a group of words that are related. Find the word <u>revolving</u> in this word ladder.

revolve
revolves
revolved
revolving
revolution

Add another word to each of the following word families.

1. circle circus circling _____	**2.** spin spins spinner _____
3. spiral spirals spiraled _____	**4.** orb orbit orbits _____
5. center central centered _____	**6.** cloud clouds clouded _____
7. sun sunny sunnier _____	**8.** star starry starfish _____

Many words have several different meanings.

The planets are <u>revolving</u> around the sun.
Be careful when you walk through a <u>revolving</u> door.

Read each pair of sentences. Think about the meaning of the underlined word or words. Circle the letter beside the meaning.

1. Sandy fixed her hair in <u>spiral</u> curls. **(A)** a circular shape **B** a square shape **C** a triangle shape	Don't let the noise <u>spiral out of control!</u> **F** spin in circles **G** turn into a circular shape **(H)** grow too loud
2. The toy top is <u>spinning</u> faster and faster. **A** flying **(B)** turning **C** jumping	It's fun to listen when Gramps starts <u>spinning a story</u>. **F** twirling a book **G** turning the pages in a book **(H)** making up a story
3. To write an *o*, you make a <u>circle</u>. **(A)** round shape **B** square shape **C** straight line	Robert and I have the same <u>circle of friends</u>. **F** friends who stand in a circle **(G)** group of friends **H** round-shaped friends

Write two sentences. Use two different meanings for <u>star</u>.

_____

_____

Name _____ **Synonyms**

These words are synonyms. They have similar meanings.

anchored   attached   connected   fastened   united

Draw a picture for each word. Label each picture with a short sentence. For example: My hand is <u>connected</u> to my arm.

1.	2.
3.	4.
5.	

Adding a prefix to a base word changes the meaning.

The string is <u>tied</u>. The string is <u>untied</u>. I have <u>retied</u> the string.

---

1. Add <u>un-</u> and <u>re-</u> to <u>attached</u> and <u>fastened</u>. Write the new words.

   _____unattached_____   _____unfastened_____

   _____reattached_____   _____refastened_____

2. Add <u>un-</u>, <u>dis-</u>, and <u>re-</u> to <u>connected</u>. Write the new words.

   _____unconnected_____   _____disconnected_____

   _____reconnected_____

3. Add <u>un-</u> to <u>anchored</u>. Add <u>re-</u> to <u>united</u>. Write the new words.

   _____unanchored_____   _____reunited_____

---

4. Draw and label pictures about two words you wrote.

Name _____

The following words have similar meanings. Their meanings are similar to "joined together" or "combined together."

anchored   attached   connected   fastened   united

The words have other meanings as well. Read the numbered sentences. Write the letter of the sentence that comes next. The first is done for you.

__C__ **1.** I'm not moving.

__D__ **2.** I'm very fond of my sister.

__E__ **3.** My friend and I agree.

__B__ **4.** The cat spies a bird.

__A__ **5.** Apples and oranges are fruit.

A. They are <u>connected</u>.

B. Her eyes are <u>fastened</u> on it.

C. I'm staying <u>anchored</u> to my desk!

D. We're very <u>attached</u> to each other.

E. We are <u>united</u>!

Choose one of the sentence pairs. Draw a picture to show what the sentences mean.

Name_____

These words are related. Some name animals. Some name people. Some name both.

beasts   beings   creatures   critters   varmints

Draw pictures to illustrate the labels.

human beings	furry creatures
annoying varmints	farm beasts
cute critters	my favorite creatures

Vocabulary Power

Name_____

We can use one word in many different ways. Beasts are animals, but sometimes we say that people act more like beasts than animals do!

Cows and horses are helpful beasts.
I think that rude people are beastly.

Add to each category. Write words. Draw pictures. Be a creative creature!

Make-Believe Critters dragons	**Creature Comforts** lots of tasty food
Ways to Act Beastly yelling in class	**Things to Say to a Varmint** shoo

People who live in different places often use different words to name the same thing. The underlined words have the same meaning. Which word do you usually say?

Horses are nice <u>animals</u>.
Horses are nice <u>critters</u>.
Horses are nice <u>beasts</u>.

Circle the word or words you use. Draw a picture.

Responses will vary.

porch lanai patio stoop	frying pan spider skillet
pancakes hotcakes flapjacks	paper bag sack tote poke

Name _____

The following words have similar meanings. They all describe
ways people can be <u>considerate</u>, or nice to each other.

mannerly   courteous   polite   thoughtful

**How do you show you are considerate? Are you mannerly,
courteous, polite, and thoughtful? Draw pictures. You can add
speech balloons, too.**

A friend is not feeling well. Show how to be <u>thoughtful</u>.	Someone has trouble opening a door. Show how to be <u>courteous</u>.
Someone gives you a gift that you don't like. Show how to be <u>polite</u>.	A family member wants to take a nap. Show how to be <u>considerate</u>.

Antonyms are words that have opposite meanings.

happy	connect	careful
unhappy	disconnect	careless

Circle the word that is the opposite of the word in dark print.

1. polite
politely
(impolite)
replace

2. courteous
courtroom
courteously
(discourteous)

3. behave
(misbehave)
behaving
act

4. thoughtful
thoughts
(thoughtless)
rethought

5. friendly
(unfriendly)
friendship
friends

6. kind
kindly
(unkind)
kindness

7. well-mannered
manners
mannerly
(ill-mannered)

8. pleased
(displeased)
pleasantly
pleasingly

9. hopeless
hoping
hopping
(hopeful)

Choose a pair of opposites. Draw and label pictures to show the meanings.

Vocabulary Power

Name_____

Words that have the same base word belong to the same word family. Underline the word friend in each of these words.

friends   friendly   unfriendly   friendship   friendless

Add prefixes and endings to the words in dark print to make word families. Possible responses are given.

1. consider	2. polite
considerate	impolite
reconsider; consideration	politeness
3. manner	**4. courteous**
mannered	discourteous
mannerly	courteously
5. thought	**6. please**
thoughtful	pleases; pleasure
thoughtfulness	pleasing; displease

Write one sentence. Use any three of the words you wrote.

_____

_____

Vocabulary Power   **Unit 4 • Chapter 19   57**

Name _____

The words in the box have similar meanings. Read the words. How do they make you feel? Hungry?

appetizing	delicious
flavorful	luscious
savory	tasty

Draw pictures to show the meaning of the underlined words. Share your pictures with classmates. Compare your ideas.

an <u>appetizing</u> breakfast	a <u>delicious</u> lunch
a <u>flavorful</u> salad	a <u>luscious</u> dessert
a <u>savory</u> dinner	a <u>tasty</u> snack

Vocabulary Power

Name _____

The following words have similar meanings. They all describe foods we enjoy—foods that look good, smell good, and taste good.

     appetizing   delicious   flavorful   luscious   savory

What foods do these words make you think of? Draw and label pictures.

sweet, creamy, cold	salty, crispy, crunchy
hot, spicy, chunky	juicy, tender, rich

Draw two of your favorite foods. Use three or more words from the box to describe each food.

sweet	creamy	crispy	hot
juicy	sour	smooth	crunchy
warm	hearty	spicy	lumpy
tender	cold	thick	salty
chunky	fluffy	icy	rich

Words that describe foods can be used to describe other things—
things that are totally different from food.

> Rock candy tastes <u>sweet</u>.
> My friend Candy is a <u>sweet</u> person.

**Draw and label pictures to answer the questions. Share your
pictures with classmates. Compare ideas.**

It's a hot, hot day. What would be a <u>luscious</u> way to get cool?	You're looking for a good book. What topic would be <u>appetizing</u>?
You've worked hard. You're tired. What would look <u>delicious</u> to you?	It's been a rough day. You're cranky. You have a <u>sour</u> look on your face.

Name _____

These words are synonyms. They have similar meanings.

   coil   swirl   twirl   twist   whirl

Draw pictures to illustrate the sentences.

The rattlesnake is coiled.	The bee swirls around the flower.
I can twirl this stick.	I can twist this rope to make a lasso.
When I dance, I like to whirl.	The chimney smoke spirals in the air.

Name _____

Rhyming words end with the same sounds. They begin with different sounds.

–ot: c̲o̲t, d̲o̲t, g̲o̲t, h̲o̲t, j̲o̲t, l̲o̲t, n̲o̲t, p̲o̲t, r̲o̲t, trot, blot, plot, sp̲o̲t

Write rhyming words for the phonograms in dark print. Start by using the letters in the ( ). Then use other letters.

-in (sp)		**-irl** (tw, wh, sw)	
spin		twirl	whirl
		swirl	
-ist (tw)		**-oil** (c)	
twist		coil	
-urn (t)		**-ing** (r)	
turn		ring	

Read all the words you wrote. Circle the word <u>spin</u>. Circle other words that have a similar meaning.

Vocabulary Power

Name _____

Sometimes two words have been blended to make another word.

twist + whirl = twirl   flash + glare = flare

Draw pictures to show the meaning of the blended words.

gleam + shimmer = glimmer	squirm + wiggle = squiggle
motor + pedal = moped	motor + hotel = motel

These words have similar meanings.
    countless
    endless
    infinite
    unlimited
    vast
	!!!!! NEWS FLASH !!!!!
	 To understand these words, it's helpful to understand the meaning of <u>limited</u>. Something that's <u>limited</u> has a beginning and an end.
	    I have 15 minutes to talk. My time is <u>limited</u>.
	    We can't all fit in this elevator. Space is <u>limited</u>.

Show the meaning of the underlined word. Draw a picture, write words, or do both. Share your ideas with classmates.

<u>limited</u>	<u>unlimited</u>
<u>infinite</u>	<u>countless</u>
<u>endless</u>	<u>vast</u>

Name _____

Words that have the same base word belong to the same word family. Underline the base word <u>agree</u> in the following words.

agreeing   agreement   disagreement   agreeable

Make new words. Circle words that have the same meaning.

1. end + ed = _____

end + ing = _____

end + less = _____

un + end + ing = _____
Circle the words that mean "without end."

2. limit + ed = _____

un + limit + ed = _____

limit + less = _____
Circle the words that mean "without limit."

3. count + s = _____

count + ing = _____

count + less = _____

count + able = _____

un + count + able = _____
Circle the words that mean "can't be counted."

Name _____

We often use words to express strong feelings.

"I am so happy today! My happiness is <u>unlimited</u>!"

Someone whose happiness is <u>unlimited</u> is very, very, very happy.

Answer the questions. Draw pictures, write, or do both.

---

1. "I have so much to do! It's <u>endless</u>!"
What has seemed <u>endless</u> to you?

---

2. "Don't slam the door. I have told you <u>countless</u> times!"
What has someone told you <u>countless</u> times?

---

3. "This is <u>infinitely</u> beautiful!"
What seems <u>infinitely</u> beautiful to you?

Vocabulary Power

Name _____

The following words are related. They describe how fast someone or something is.

hasty   quicker   rapid   speedily   swiftness

Draw pictures to show the meaning of the words in dark print. Write a sentence to describe each picture.

1. quicker
2. rapid
3. hasty
4. swiftness
5. speedily

Name _____

These words belong to the same word family.

haste: hasty   hastily   hastiest   hastiness

Add endings to the words in dark print to make word families.

Possible responses are given.

1. quick _quickly_ _quickest_ _quicken_	**2.** speed _speedy_ _speedily_ _speediness_
3. rapid _rapidly_ _rapidness_ _____	**4.** swift _swiftly_ _swifter_ _swiftest_
5. slow _slowness_ _slowly_ _slowing_	**6.** slack _slackness_ _slacken_ _slackly_

Which two base words mean the opposite of <u>quick</u>?

_____slow_____   _____slack_____

Name _____

Words that have similar meanings are called <u>synonyms</u>.

quick—fast   quicker—faster   quickness—fastness

Read the word in dark print. Circle the letter beside the synonym.

1. speedier A slow B faster C quickest D fasten	**2. swiftness** A quickly B slowness C rapid D quickness	**3. quicker** A haste B runner C swifter D slower
4. rapidly A quickly B hurry C zoom D quicker	**5. hasty** A slow B silly C fast D jog	**6. swiftly** A speed B slackly C faster D rapidly
7. quickness A running B speediness C speeder D speedier	**8. speedily** A hastily B vastly C swifter D unlimited	**9. quick** A fasten B slowly C speedy D swiftness
10. slowness A restful B slackness C quickness D sleepiness	**11. huge** A tiniest B wildly C vast D unforgettable	**12. swirly** A squarely B roundness C untwist D whirly

Context clues can help you understand the meaning of unfamiliar words. Use clues in this sentence to help you understand the meaning of <u>royal</u>.

The king and queen are members of the <u>royal</u> family.

Use context clues to help you understand the meaning of the underlined word. Draw a picture to illustrate the meaning.

1. You have to dress up. The party is <u>formal</u>.	**2.** Everyone at the party wore their best clothes. They looked <u>regal</u>.
3. My friend always looks and acts very well. She's quite <u>dignified</u>.	**4.** I gave up my seat to let Gramps sit down. He said I was <u>noble</u>.

Name _____

There are times when it is fine to be informal. There are other
times when you are expected to be formal and dignified. Read
the sentences. Write the category—Formal, Informal.

Informal	Formal
Hi!	Hello.
What's up?	I'm very pleased to meet you.
Howdy!	How do you do?
Hey!	Pardon me.
So long!	Excuse me, please.
Thanks.	Thank you very much.

Draw and label pictures for the following categories.

Formal Clothes

Informal Clothes

How to Act Dignified

There are many different titles for people.

President   **King**   **Duke**   **Officer**
Vice President **Queen**   **Duchess**   **Professor**
Ambassador   **Princess** **Countess** **Principal**

Write titles from above for each category below. Then add another title. Use art paper to draw a picture to illustrate one of the titles in each box.

Royal, or Regal, Titles	Government Titles
King	President
Queen	Vice President
Princess	Ambassador

Titles of Nobles	Work Titles
Duke	Officer
Duchess	Professor
Countess	Principal

Name _____   **Word Families**

Words in the same word family have related meanings. Draw a line from each word in dark print to other words in the same word family.

action ·   · contribute, contributed
connection ·   · predict, predicting
contribution ·   · act, acted, acting
prediction ·   · transport, transports
transportation ·   · connect, connected

Draw pictures to show the meaning of the underlined words.

1. a silly <u>action</u>	**2.** a weather <u>prediction</u>
3. an important <u>connection</u>	**4.** a large <u>contribution</u>
5. forms of <u>transportation</u>	

A <u>suffix</u>, or ending, can be added to a verb to make a noun.

When you <u>collect</u> things, you have a <u>collection</u>.
collect + -ion = collection

If you <u>recommend</u> a book, you are giving a <u>recommendation</u>.
recommend + -ation = recommendation

Add -ion to each underlined verb. Then write the noun to complete the sentence. (Don't forget that for some words, you have to drop the final e before adding an ending.)

I. If you <u>connect</u> two things, you make a _____.

2. If you <u>predict</u> something, you make a _____.

3. If you <u>contribute</u> something, you make a _____.

4. If you <u>communicate</u>, you have _____.

5. If people <u>act</u>, you have _____.

Add -ation to each underlined verb. Then write the noun to complete the sentence.

6. When you <u>converse</u>, you have a _____.

7. To <u>transport</u> something, you need _____.

8. If you <u>limit</u> something, you make a _____.

Name _____ **Analogies**

An <u>analogy</u> is a word puzzle. Think about how the first two words are related.

<u>formal</u>–<u>informal</u>   is like   unhappy–_____

The words <u>formal</u> and <u>informal</u> are opposites.

What is the opposite of <u>unhappy</u>?

Complete each puzzle. Choose one of the words under the blank and write it on the line.

1. <u>contribute</u>–<u>contribution</u> is like <u>act</u>–_____ action nation sleep	**2.** <u>look</u>–<u>observe</u> is like talk–_____ connect converse yawn
3. <u>Saturday</u>–<u>day</u> is like March–_____ week year month	**4.** <u>truck</u>–<u>transportation</u> is like <u>squirrel</u>–_____ plant animal action
5. <u>hat</u>–<u>cap</u> is like prediction–_____ guess fact connection	**6.** <u>connected</u>–<u>apart</u> is like sweet–_____ salty delicious sour
7. <u>basket</u>–<u>straw</u> is like jeans–_____ metal cloth wood	**8.** <u>water</u>–<u>sea</u> is like sand–_____ dry desert ocean

Name _____

These words are synonyms. They have similar meanings.

frayed   ragged   shaggy   tattered   uneven

**Draw a picture to show the meaning of the word in dark print.
Label your picture. For example: a shaggy dog.**

1. frayed	**2.** ragged
3. shaggy	**4.** tattered
5. uneven	**6.** even

Vocabulary Power

Name_____

Which sayings have you heard? What do they mean?

look like a Raggedy-Ann   even–Steven

Draw pictures to show what these sayings mean.

1. shaggy dog look	**2.** uneven numbers
3. ragged corners	**4.** frayed cuffs

Make up your own saying.

_____

Name _____

Some rhyming words have similar spellings. Others have different spellings.

road   load   sewed   code   showed

Some words that have similar spellings don't rhyme.

hugged–rugged   some–home   have–save

Write rhyming words for the word in dark print. Some of the words may have a different spelling. Remember: Words with similar spellings may or may not rhyme.

Possible responses include:

1. tatter	2. frayed
spatter, matter, flatter	made, maid, stayed
scatter, batter, patter	paid, played, weighed
3. lagged	**4. shaggy**
wagged, bagged, sagged	baggy, saggy, raggy
dragged, tagged, nagged	Maggie, Aggie, craggy
5. ragged	**6. even**
jagged	Steven

Name _____

These words are related because they all have to do with teaching or explaining something.

demonstrate   display   illustrate   model   present

Draw pictures to show the meaning of the underlined words.

1. I can demonstrate how to dance.	**2.** I can display my favorite books.
3. I can illustrate ways to tie knots.	**4.** I can model how to add numbers.
5. I can present a book report.	**6.** This is my favorite teacher.

Name _____

Some words have many different meanings.

The buttons are <u>attached</u> to the coat.
My friend and I are very <u>attached</u>.

Write the word in dark print to complete each phrase. Circle one of the phrases and draw a picture to show its meaning.

---

1. illustrate

_____ a picture

_____ a dance

---

2. model

_____ a coat

make a _____

---

3. display

present a _____

_____ happiness

---

4. present

_____ a report

_____ a prize

Vocabulary Power

Name _____

Homographs are words that have the same spelling, but they are pronounced differently and they have different meanings.

> I'm keeping a <u>record</u> of different birds I see.
> Let's use this tape to <u>record</u> some music.

Draw pictures to show the meaning of the underlined words.

1. This <u>present</u> is for you.	**2.** We will <u>present</u> a play.
3. <u>Wind</u> the clock.	**4.** The <u>wind</u> is blowing.
5. <u>Lead</u> the parade.	**6.** <u>Lead</u> is a kind of metal.

Name _____

These words are related because they all have something to do with teaching or leading.

advise   direct   guided   led   taught

Write or draw to demonstrate the meaning of the underlined word.

1. I <u>led</u> the way.	**2.** The signs <u>guided</u> me home.
3. The officer will <u>direct</u> traffic.	**4.** Who <u>taught</u> you how to read?
5. I will <u>advise</u> you when to stop.	**6.** Please <u>direct</u> me to the gym.

Name _____

Some words can be used in many different ways.

> You can run. You can hit a home run.
> You can be a model. You can model how to skip.

Read the sentence pairs. Think about the meanings of the underlined words. Then follow the directions.

---

1. Dad has to park the car. We are visiting a wildlife park. Show or describe what a wildlife park is.

---

2. The signs direct us to the park. This path is the most direct. Show or describe a direct path.

---

3. The man can guide us. He is a park guide. Show or describe what a park guide does.

---

4. The guide taught us birdsongs. The lesson was well-taught. Show or describe what well-taught means.

Vocabulary Power

Name _____

Homophones are words that sound the same, but they have different spellings and different meanings.

read–reed   loan–lone   seam–seem   taught–taut

Draw and label pictures to illustrate the meanings of these homophones.

1. led–lead
2. road–rode
3. write–right
4. grown–groan

Vocabulary Power

Name _____

These words describe ways you can do something.

angrily   gracefully   hungrily   noisily   playfully

Use the context clues to help you understand the meaning of the underlined words. Answer the questions by drawing or writing.

1. The dancers move <u>gracefully</u>. What can you do gracefully?	**2.** The cat watches the bird <u>hungrily</u>. What do you look at hungrily?
3. The dogs bark <u>noisily</u>. What can you do noisily?	**4.** The baby gurgles <u>playfully</u>. What can you do playfully?
5. Bees buzz <u>angrily</u>. What else buzzes angrily?	**6.** The fish swam <u>gracefully</u>. What else moves gracefully?

A suffix is an ending that is added to a base word. Some words have one suffix. Other words have two suffixes.

anger + y = angry   anger + y + ly = angrily
play + ful = playful   play + ful + ly = playfully

1. Add the following suffixes: y y + ly	**2.** Add the following suffixes: ful ful + ly
speed speedy speedily	**grace** graceful gracefully
noise noisy noisily	**hope** hopeful hopefully
anger angry angrily	**rest** restful restfully
hunger hungry hungrily	**help** helpful helpfully

Name _____

Antonyms are words that have opposite meanings.

    give–take   sink–float   empty–full

Write an antonym for each word. Use the words in the box.

noisy	**slow**	**playful**	**polite**
graceful	**unsteady**	**noisily**	**slowly**
playfully	**politely**	**gracefully**	**unsteadily**

1. clumsy – _____   clumsily – _____

2. quiet – _____   quietly – _____

3. serious – _____   seriously – _____

4. swift – _____   swiftly – _____

5. steady – _____   steadily – _____

6. rude – _____   rudely – _____

Choose two pairs of antonyms. Draw and label pictures to show the opposite meanings.

Name _____

Read the following words. Circle the words you know.

interact intercom interleaf international Internet

For boxes 1–5, use context clues to figure out the meaning of the underlined word. Draw or write to answer the question. For box 6, answer the question. Accept reasonable responses.

1. When people <u>interact</u>, they communicate. What are some ways in which people interact?	**2.** I use my computer to find things on the <u>Internet</u>. What do you know about the Internet?
3. Everyone in the world sings. Singing is <u>international</u>. What other things are international?	**4.** This book has an <u>interleaf</u> at the end. It is blank on the front and back. What is an interleaf?
5. The principal talked to us over the <u>intercom</u>. What is an intercom? Does your classroom have one?	**6.** Look at the words you circled at the top of the page. Did you learn anything new about the words? What?

These words begin with the same prefix. Underline inter- in each word.

interact   intercom   interleaf   international   Internet

Complete each sentence. Use a word from above.

1. Something known among many nations is

_____international_____.

2. When people talk among themselves, they

_____interact_____.

3. A blank page at the beginning or end of a book is called an

_____interleaf_____.

Add inter- to the words. Draw pictures for labels.

1. connected	2. twined
_____interconnected_____ telephones	_____intertwined_____ ropes

Name _____

A clipped word is like an abbreviation. It's a short form of a longer word.

intercom — intercommunication

An intercom is a machine used for communication.

internet — internetwork

The Internet is a group of computer networks.

Write the clipped words for these longer words. Draw pictures.

1. automobile _____auto_____	**2.** airplane _____plane_____
3. telephone _____phone_____	**4.** eyeglasses _____glasses_____
5. catcher's mitten catcher's _____mitt_____	**6.** recreation room _____rec_____ room

Vocabulary Power

Name _____

These compound words are the names of animals.

anteater   groundhog   mockingbird   starfish   stingray

Use the animal names to help you complete the sentences. Draw pictures of the animals.

1. An anteater eats _____ .	**2.** If you step on a stingray, you will get a _____ .
3. A mockingbird _____ the sounds of other birds.	**4.** A starfish is shaped like a _____ .

5. A groundhog lives in the _____ .

Name _____

These animals can be grouped into many different categories.

anteater   groundhog   mockingbird   starfish   stingray

Write the animal names above in at least one category. Add other animal names to complete each category. Additional responses will vary.

BIRDS	FISH
mockingbird	starfish
	stingray

MAMMALS	ANIMALS THAT FLY
anteater	mockingbird
groundhog	

ANIMALS THAT EAT INSECTS	ANIMALS THAT STING
anteater	stingray

The same animal can have different names in different places.

Which name do you use? groundhog or woodchuck?

Read the words. Circle the word or words you use. Draw a picture.

1. peanuts goobers ground nuts	**2.** sub hoagie grinder
3. soda tonic pop	**4.** spuds potatoes taters

Name _____

These words are related because they all name sounds.

bellow   croak   hoot   warble   yowl

For boxes 1–5, read the sentence and draw a picture of an animal that makes the sound. For box 6, draw a picture showing when you might make one of the sounds.

1. A <u>bellow</u> is deep and roaring.	**2.** A <u>croak</u> is low and hoarse.
3. A <u>hoot</u> is a kind of cry.	**4.** A <u>warble</u> is song-like.
5. A <u>yowl</u> is a kind of whine.	**6.** I can _____.

Name _____ **Onomatopoeia**

There are many words that describe sounds.

bellow   croak   hoot   warble   yowl

Write the above sounds in the following categories. Add other words to complete each category.

LOUD SOUNDS	QUIET SOUNDS	GRUFF SOUNDS
bang	hush	grunt
_____	_____	_____
_____	_____	_____
_____	_____	_____
_____	_____	_____

ANIMAL SOUNDS	WEATHER SOUNDS	MUSIC SOUNDS
yowl	whoosh	toot-toot
_____	_____	_____
_____	_____	_____
_____	_____	_____

Name_____

Which words are more descriptive? Why?

"Hurray," Mitchell said.   "Ouch," Joan said.
"Hurray," Mitchell bellowed.   "Ouch," Joan yowled.

Substitute another word for said. Write the word on the blank. Draw a picture to illustrate the sentence. Share your ideas with classmates. Possible responses are given. Accept reasonable responses.

1. "Let's play ball," said Juan. ___shouted___	**2.** "I'm late," said Doris. ___sighed___
3. "What time is it?" said Raj. ___asked___	**4.** "Help, help!" said Barnie. ___screamed___
5. "Oink, oink," said the pig. ___squealed___	**6.** "Grrr, grrr," said the bear. ___growled___

Name _____

These words in dark print are related because they all have
something to do with communication.

correspondence e-mail memo message post

Draw pictures or write descriptions to illustrate the meaning of
each word.

1. message	**2.** e-mail
3. post	**4.** memo
5. correspondence	

Name _____

A clipped word is a shortened form of a longer word.

telephone—phone   eyeglasses—glasses

Write the clipped words for these longer words. Write or draw pictures to explain the meanings.

1. memorandum _memo_	**2.** electronic mail _e-mail_
3. stereophonic _stereo_	**4.** gymnasium _gym_
5. rhinoceros _rhino_	**6.** hippopotamus _hippo_

Vocabulary Power

<u>Jargon</u> is language that is used by a group of people who do the same work or have the same interests. People who work with computers or who are interested in computers use jargon.

Brainstorm things that are related to computers. Add to the items in the box.

e-mail   post a message

Other computer words or phrases:

reasonable resources

_____   mouse   _____   _____

_____   keyboard   _____   _____

_____   crash   _____   _____

Now draw and label pictures.

Name _____

These words are synonyms. They have similar meanings.

fabulous   fantastic   marvelous   splendid   superb

Draw or write to illustrate the meaning of the underlined words.

1. a <u>fabulous</u> place to visit	**2.** a <u>fantastic</u> TV show
3. a <u>marvelous</u> dinner	**4.** a <u>splendid</u> bicycle
5. a <u>superb</u> time	**6.** a <u>marvelous</u> birthday

Name _____

The origin of a word is the word's history.

The word lasso comes from a Spanish word for rope.

The word in dark print comes from another word. What do you think the other word means? Circle the letter beside the meaning that makes sense.

1. fabulous **A** an old word for fable **B** an old word for sad **C** an old word for hurry **D** an old word for information	**2. splendid** **A** an old word for terrible **B** an old word for green **C** an old word for shine **D** an old word for frozen
3. fantastic **A** an old word for rabbit **B** an old word for make-believe **C** an old word for fan **D** an old word for impolite	**4. cocoon** **A** an old word for shell **B** an old word for raccoon **C** an old word for cocoa **D** an old word for cork
5. royal **A** an old word for gown **B** an old word for cheese **C** an old word for king **D** an old word for day	**6. delve** **A** an old word for climb **B** an old word for go **C** an old word for stop **D** an old word for dig

An analogy is a word puzzle. Think about how the first two words are related. Think of a word related to the third word in the same way.

bicycle–two is like tricycle–_____
A bicycle has two wheels. How many wheels does a tricycle have?

Complete these word puzzles. Share your answers.

1. fabulous–wonderful is like mad–_____ angry

2. horse–trot is like frog–_____ hop, leap, jump

3. lumpy–smooth is like awful–_____ great, marvelous

4. fifteen–number is like purple–_____ color

5. bellow–loud is like whisper–_____ soft, quiet

6. tremble–shiver is like splendid–_____ great, wonderful

7. memorandum–memo is like internetwork–_____ internet

8. corn–vegetable is like tulip–_____ flower

9. calf–cow is like cub–_____ bear

10. France–country is like Texas–_____ state

11. quickly–quick is like superbly–_____ superb

12. honey–sweet is like lemon–_____ sour

Name _____

Synonyms have similar meanings. Antonyms have opposite meanings. Which word pairs are synonyms? Which are antonyms?

happy — glad   first — beginning   stop — halt
happy — sad   first — last   stop — go

Use the synonyms to help you understand the meaning of the word in dark print. Draw a picture to illustrate the meaning.

1. bolt — hurry — dash	**2. plunge** — dive — jump
3. scamper — run — rush	**4. linger** — stay — dilly-dally

Use the antonyms to help you understand the meaning of the word in dark print. Draw a picture to illustrate the meaning.

5. dawdle — scamper — rush

Name _____

These words name ways to move.

bolt   dawdle   linger   plunge   scamper

Read these descriptions. Do you picture something moving fast or slowly?

a scampering kitten   a plunging kite

a dawdling snail   lingering smoke

a bolting horse   a bolt of lightning

dawdling ducks   scampering children

Write the descriptions above in the correct box. Add other descriptions.

FAST	SLOW
a scampering kitten	a dawdling snail
a bolting horse	dawdling ducks
a plunging kite	lingering smoke
a bolt of lightning	
scampering children	

               Vocabulary Power

Context clues can help you understand different meanings of the same word.

> Hurry! We have to <u>dash</u>.
> Write a <u>dash</u> between the words.

Draw pictures or write to show the meaning of the underlined words.

1. The mice <u>scamper</u> into their nest.	**2.** Hurry, Jan. We have to <u>scamper</u>!
3. The penguins <u>plunge</u> into the icy water.	**4.** Let's try something new. Let's take a <u>plunge</u>.
5. The dogs <u>bolt</u> out of the yard.	**6.** Don't forget to <u>bolt</u> the door.

These words all mean "to do something again."

recount   recycle   rethink   retrace   review

Read the sentences. Use the context clues to figure out the meanings of the underlined words. Write or draw pictures to explain the meanings.

1. We are lost. We have to retrace our steps.	**2.** I'm saving these old newspapers. They can be recycled.
3. I can tell you what happened. I will recount the events.	**4.** This plan will not work. We have to rethink our ideas.
5. We're having a spelling test. Let's review our spelling words.	**6.** You counted 20, and I counted 22. We have to do a recount.

Name _____

These words start with the same prefix. Underline re- in each word.

rethink means "to think again"   recount means "to count again"
retrace means "to trace again"   review means "to view again"

**Add re- to each word. Write or draw a picture to explain
the meaning of the new word.**

1. use _____reuse_____	**2.** turn _____return_____
3. write _____rewrite_____	**4.** unite _____reunite_____
5. paint _____repaint_____	**6.** read _____reread_____
7. heat _____reheat_____	**8.** play _____replay_____

Name _____

When things are <u>recycled</u>, they are reused.

Old newspapers can be <u>recycled</u> to make new paper.
A broken table can be <u>recycled</u> by repairing it.

Brainstorm ideas for each category. Write or draw pictures to express your ideas. Share your ideas with classmates.
Accept reasonable responses.

THINGS THAT CAN BE RECYCLED	WAYS TO RECYCLE THINGS

Possible responses:
glass bottles
plastic containers
plastic bags
newspapers
magazines
white paper
aluminum/soda cans
egg crates
	Possible responses:
	deliver to recycling plant
	reuse in creative ways
	use refills instead of buying
	    complete products again
	    e.g. juices
	buy products made of
	    recycled paper/plastic

Glossary

ac·tion [ak′shən] Waving hello is a friendly *action*.

a·dult [ə·dult′ or ad′ult] An *adult* is a grown-up.

ad·vise [ad·vīz′] Our teachers *advise* us to study for tests.

a·gree·ment [ə·grē′mənt] We reached *agreement* that we all should go.

am·bas·sa·dor [am·bas′ə·dər *or* am·bas′ə·dôr] She is an *ambassador* for world peace.

an·chored [ang′kərd] They *anchored* the young tree to the ground with wires.

an·gri·ly [ang′grə·lē] He frowned and stomped away *angrily*.

ant·eat·er [ant′ē·tər] The *anteater* uses its long snout to scoop up ants.

an·them [an′thəm] "The Star-Spangled Banner" is our national *anthem*.

ap·pe·tiz·ing [ap′ə·tī·zing] That pizza looks very *appetizing* to eat.

at·tached [ə·tacht′] I *attached* photos to my report.

beasts [bēsts] The wild *beasts* of the forest rested in the shade.

be·ings [bē′ingz] We are all human *beings*.

bel·low [bel′ō] He gave a loud *bellow* when the dog knocked him down.

bolt [bōlt] The racers *bolt* to the finish line.

bright•est [brīt′əst] One of the *brightest* stars is the North Star.

bron•co [brong′kō] The ranchers chased the wild *bronco* into the stable.

bur•row [bûr′ō] The rabbits are safe underground in their *burrow*.

C

cap•ture [kap′chər] I want to *capture* that insect and take it outside.

cat•e•gor•y [kat′ə•gôr•ē] In what *category* or group would you place this story?

cat•tail [kat′tāl] Tall *cattail* plants grow next to the pond.

cave [kāv] Bears hibernate in that *cave*.

chair•per•son [châr′pûr•sən] We elect a new *chairperson* at every meeting.

cir•cu•lar [sûr′kyə•lər] I stirred the soup with a *circular* motion.

clutch [kluch] The baby likes to *clutch* her blanket in her tiny hands.

co•coons [kə•kōōnz′] The moths emerged from their *cocoons*.

coil [koil] Sailors *coil* ropes into circles on the ship's deck.

com•mu•ni•cate [kə•myōō′nə•kāt] We write letters to *communicate* with our friends.

con•fer [kən•fûr′] We will *confer* with the principal about that rule.

con•nec•ted [kə•nek′təd] The bridge *connected* the two islands.

con·nec·tion [kə·nek′shən] What is the *connection* between lions and cats?

con·sid·er·ate [kən·sid′ər·it] It was *considerate* of you to help me with my chores.

con·sul·ting [kən·sul′ting] The nurse is *consulting* the doctor about my fever.

con·tri·bu·tion [kon·trə·byoo′shən] The principal thanked us for our *contribution* to the school.

con·verse [kən·vûrs′] I *converse* loudly with my friends at lunchtime.

cor·re·spon·dence [kôr·ə·spon′dəns] She saved all the letters from her *correspondence* with her penpal.

count·less [kount′lis] They worked for *countless* hours to finish the project on time.

coun·try·side [kun′trē·sīd] Spring is most beautiful in the *countryside*.

cour·te·ous [kûr′tē·əs] Our hosts were *courteous* and polite.

cow·hand [kou′hand] The *cowhand* drove the cattle to the pasture.

crea·tures [krē′chərz] All *creatures* need food, water, and shelter to survive.

crit·ters [krit′ərz] The vet held the furry little *critters* carefully in her hands.

croak [krōk] We could hear the frog's *croak* from across the pond.

cy·cle [sī′kəl] The life *cycle* of the butterfly has three different stages.

D

daw•dle [dôd′əl] My dad doesn't like me to *dawdle* when he's in a hurry.

de•li•cious [di•lish′əs] I would like some more of that *delicious* fruit salad.

delve [delv] Our research group will *delve* into books about desert life.

dem•on•strate [dem′ən•strāt] Terry will *demonstrate* how to hit the ball.

dig•ni•fied [dig′nə•fīd] The guests at the banquet were polite and *dignified*.

di•rect [di•rekt′ *or* dī•rekt′] Sometimes we need someone to *direct* traffic in the hallways.

dis•a•gree•ment [dis•ə•grē′mənt] They settled their *disagreement* and became friends.

dis•har•mon•y [dis•här′mə•nē] When people argue, there is *disharmony*.

dis•play [dis•plā′] 1. The runners will *display* their speed. 2. The grocer made a *display* of fresh fruits.

E

e-mail [ē•māl] It's fun to get *e-mail* from other schools.

end•less [end′lis] The ocean seemed *endless* to the ship's passengers.

en•tire•ly [in•tīr′lē] The painter filled the canvas *entirely* with color.

ex•plored [ik•splôrd′] The children *explored* their grandparents' barn.

F

fab•u•lous [fab′yə•ləs] They looked *fabulous* in their fancy clothes.

fam·il·y [fam′ə·lē *or* fam′lē] All our aunts, uncles, and cousins are part of our *family*.

fan·tas·tic [fan·tas′tik] He told a *fantastic* tale about traveling through space.

farm·land [färm′land] The *farmland* was plowed before seeds were planted.

fast·ened [fas′ənd] They *fastened* the boards with wood glue and nails.

field [fēld] They planted oats in the empty *field*.

fla·vor·ful [flā′vər·fəl] The stew was thick and tasted *flavorful*.

flick·er [flik′ər] The candle flame began to *flicker* before it went out.

flut·ter [flut′ər] He watched the laundry *flutter* in the breeze.

folk song [fōk sông] Our class sang a *folk song* on International Day.

for·mal [fôr′məl] They wore their best clothes to the *formal* event.

frayed [frād] The cuffs of the old shirt were worn and *frayed*.

G

gloss·i·est [glôs′ē·əst] They used the *glossiest* paper they had for the magazine's shiny cover.

grab [grab] It's not polite to *grab* something from someone.

grace·ful·ly [grās′fəl·ē] The skaters moved *gracefully* over the ice.

grasp [grasp] He will *grasp* the handle firmly to pick up the heavy suitcase.

ground·hog [ground′hog *or* ground′hôg] The *groundhog* builds its home underground.

guid·ed [gīd′əd] The teacher *guided* her students through the museum.

H

har·mo·ny [här′mə·nē] The people lived in peace and *harmony*.

hast·y [hās′tē] They ate a *hasty* dinner before rushing to the game.

hoot [hōōt] The campers hear an owl's *hoot* at night.

hun·gri·ly [hung′grə·lē] The seals looked *hungrily* at the bucket of fish.

I

il·lus·trate [il′ə·strāt] She gave an example to *illustrate* her point.

in·fi·nite [in′fə·nit] Space looks like it is *infinite* and goes on forever.

in·quire [in·kwīr′] She wrote to *inquire* about a job she wanted.

in·ter·act [in·tər·act′] We *interact* differently with friends and strangers.

in·ter·com [in′tər·com] The principal made an announcement over the *intercom*.

in·ter·leaf [in·tər·lēf′] The *interleaf* is the blank page at the end of this book.

in·ter·na·tion·al [in·tər·nash′ən·əl] There was food from five countries at the *international* dinner.

In·ter·net [in'tər·net] We can use the computer to get information from the *Internet*.

jin·gle [jing'gəl] She sang the ad's catchy *jingle* to herself.

lair [lâr] The bobcat brought its catch back to its *lair*.

lar·vae [lär'vē] Caterpillars are the *larvae* of butterflies.

las·so [las'ō] The cowboy throws a *lasso* to catch stray cows.

led [led] I *led* my little brother home.

lin·ger [lin'gər] Don't *linger* outside, or you may miss the start of the movie.

lodge [loj] The beaver lives in a *lodge* made of sticks at the edge of the pond.

lull·a·by [lul'ə·bī] Mom sang a *lullaby* to help me fall asleep.

lus·cious [lush'əs] We ate some tasty, *luscious* strawberries.

man·ner·ly [man'ər·lē] The *mannerly* children waited quietly for the show to begin.

mar·vel·ous [mär'vəl·əs] We had a *marvelous* time at the circus!

may·or [mā'ər] The leader of a city or town is called the *mayor*.

mead·ow [med'ō] The sheep eat the grass in the *meadow*.

mem·o [mem'ō] My teacher wrote a *memo* to parents about the class play.

mes·sage [mes′ij] Did you get the *message* I sent to you?

mock·ing·bird [mok′ing·bûrd] A *mockingbird* can copy the sounds of other birds.

mod·el [mod′əl] The teacher will *model* how to add the two large numbers.

most·ly [mōst′lē] On our hike, we saw *mostly* pine trees and small bushes.

N

no·ble [nō′bəl] Mom said I was *noble* when I gave my little sister the last cookie.

nois·i·ly [noi′zə·lē] The dog barks *noisily* at the cat.

O

ob·serve [əb·zûrv′] We *observe* the ants to see how they live.

of·fi·cer [of′ə·sər] The police *officer* told us to wear bike helmets.

or·bit [ôr′bit] It takes the Earth a full year to make one *orbit* around the sun.

P

part·ly [pärt′lē] The sky is *partly* cloudy.

pas·ture [pas′chər] Do you see cows eating grass in the *pasture*?

pig·tail [pig′tāl] My friend can brush her hair into one big *pigtail*.

play·ful·ly [plā′fəl·lē] My kitten *playfully* bats the toy with its paw.

plunge [plunj] The seals splash when they *plunge* into the water.

po·lite [pə·līt′] It is *polite* to say "please" when you ask for something.

post [pōst] Please *post* these messages by the door.

pre·dic·tion [pri·dik'shən] My *prediction* is that the weather will be sunny today.

pre·sent [pri·zent'] I *present* this ribbon to you for winning the race.

pres·i·dent [prez'ə·dənt] In many countries, the leader is called a *president*.

pu·pa [py$\overline{oo}$'pə] When a caterpillar is in a cocoon, it is called a *pupa*.

Q

quest [kwest] The explorer went on a *quest* to find the treasure.

quick·er [kwik'ər] A dog is *quicker* than a turtle.

quiv·er [kwiv'ər] The scary sound made me shake and *quiver*.

R

rag·ged [rag'id] The old shirt was *ragged* and full of holes.

rap·id [rap'id] The *rapid* rush of water washed away part of the road.

rat·tle·snake [rat'əl·snāk] A *rattlesnake* has fangs and a noisy tail.

rec·om·mend [rek·ə·mend'] I *recommend* that you read this great book.

re·count [rē·kount'] *Recount* the cookies to make sure you have one for each person. [ri·kount'] My grandpa likes to *recount* the story of how he met my grandma.

re·cy·cled [rē·sī'kəld] We *recycled* our old cans and glass bottles.

re·gal [rē′gəl] The king looked *regal* in his gold crown and red robe.

re·think [rē·thingk′] Let's *rethink* this problem and come up with a better idea.

re·trace [rē·trās′] I will *retrace* my steps to find my way back home.

re·view [ri·vyoo′] Today we will *review* the words we learned yesterday.

re·volv·ing [ri·volv′ing] We were dizzy when we got off the *revolving* ride.

ro·de·o [rō′dē·ō] Cowboys ride horses and bulls at the *rodeo.*

roost [roost] The birds always *roost* up on that branch.

roy·al [roi′əl] The *royal* guard protects the queen and her castle.

S

sad·dle [sad′əl] Sit tall in the *saddle* when you ride a horse.

sa·vor·y [sā′vər·ē] The *savory* food tasted as good as it smelled.

scam·per [skam′pər] The squirrels *scamper* quickly up the tree.

seize [sēz] *Seize* the handle, and climb up into the truck.

ser·e·nade [ser·ə·nād′] Jack sang a sweet *serenade* under Karen's window.

shag·gy [shag′ē] My hair looked *shaggy* and messy before I got it cut.

shin·i·est [shī′nē·əst] That bright, sparkly star is the *shiniest* one in the sky.

shiv•er [shivʹər] I always *shiver* and shake when I'm cold.

sim•i•lar [simʹə•lər] Bikes and tricycles are *similar* because both have wheels.

sleek•est [slēkʹəst] The cat's fur feels *sleekest* after I brush it.

smooth•est [smōōthʹəst] This is the *smoothest* road now that all the holes are fixed.

spe•cies [spēʹshēz *or* spēʹsēz] Are alligators an endangered *species?*

spec•i•men [spesʹə•mən] This is a fine *specimen* of a tiger shark.

speed•i•ly [spēdʹə•lē] The train ran *speedily* down the track.

spin•ning [spinʹing] She is *spinning* around and around as she plays.

spi•ral [spīʹrəl] Be careful when you walk up the winding *spiral* stairs.

splen•did [splenʹdid] The dancers wore *splendid* costumes of gold and silver.

sput•ter [sputʹər] The fire will *sputter* out if the water boils over.

star•fish [stärʹfish] We saw *starfish* with five legs in the ocean.

steer [stir] The *steer* looked a lot like the bull we saw on the farm.

sting•ray [stingʹrā] The *stingray* swims fast with its flat body and long tail.

su•perb [sŏŏ•pûrbʹ] The party was *superb* and everyone had a wonderful time.

swift·est [swift′əst] Ira was the *swiftest* runner and won the race.

swirl [swûrl] We watched the water *swirl* down the drain like a little tornado.

T

tat·tered [tat′ərd] That old coat is all *tattered* and torn.

taught [tôt] The teacher *taught* us how to spell correctly.

thought·ful [thôt′fəl] It was *thoughtful* of you to send me a get-well card.

to·geth·er·ness [tə·geth′ər·nəs] We had a lot of *togetherness* with all ten of us at home.

to·tal·ly [tōt′əl·ē] We are *totally* and completely happy with our new house.

trans·por·ta·tion [trans·pər·tā′shən] The city buses and taxis provide good *transportation*.

tur·tle·neck [tûr′təl·nek] The *turtleneck* sweater kept my neck warm in the cold weather.

twirl [twûrl] Mindy likes to *twirl* around and around on the dance floor.

twist [twist] I will *twist* your hair into a bun.

U

un·e·ven [un·ē′vən] The edges of the paper are *uneven* because I cut it too fast.

u·nit·ed [yoo·nī′tid] Our voices *united* as we sang together.

un·lim·it·ed [un·lim′it·id] The field is so huge that the dog had *unlimited* space for running.

V

var•mints [vär′mənts] Those mice and other *varmints* are eating from my garden!

vast [vast] You can see water all around in the *vast* ocean.

W

war•ble [wôr′bəl] The bird's *warble* sounds beautiful!

whirl [hwûrl] Did you see the dancers *whirl* and spin around to the fast music?

whol•ly [hō′lē] I *wholly* and completely agree that we should go camping.

Y

yowl [youl] A cat will *yowl* if you step on its tail.

My Own Word List

My Own Word List

My Own Word List